18 DAYS
BRAIN TRAINING
3/3

Enduring Brainpower!

www.alexanderhalm.de

18 DAYS BRAIN TRAINING 3/3

Enduring Brainpower!

Alexander Halm

ISBN 9798679042612

Independently published

www.alexanderhalm.de

Place of publication: Alexander Halm - Schweinsdorf 64 - 91616 Neusitz

Please visit the website www.alexanderhalm.de for further contact information.

What's your own motto for this book?

"_____

_____

_____ "

CONTENTS

HOW TO USE THIS BOOK

READ THIS BEFORE YOU START!

After two books you are already a brain training expert! This volume will help you to deepen your skills so that you have the chance that your achieved performance will stay at the same level for longer. In order to stay fit, however, you should also do some memory training exercises regularly after working with this book.

The tasks of the units are about as difficult as in the previous book.

If you haven't worked with the second volume, you will get an introduction to the deciphering tasks on the next few pages.

Do you already know how to decrypt them? Then you can skip this and start your workout right away with day 1!

I wish you a lot of fun and success!

HOW TO USE THIS BOOK

DECIPHERING TASKS

It's easy to decipher the codes in this book once you know how to do it!

You have to work them row by row from top to bottom. Here you can see the processing sequence for the example on the right from a) to f):

a) Add the two numbers of line 2 and 3.	$2 + 7 = 9$
b) Write the result in the gap below (line 4).	9
c) Find the letter from line 1 in the alphabet printed below and add the previous result to the right.	$S + 9 = A$
d) Write the character you found in the space under the total number (line 5).	Write "A" under the calculated sum.
e) Line 6 specifies the place where the character appears in the original text.	For the first column it is 3.
f) Write the character from line 5 in the correct place in line 7.	Write "A" in the placeholder 3.

Did you understand everything? Then try now to solve the rest of the example yourself.

If you need more help, see pages 12 and 13.

HOW TO USE THIS BOOK

The lines for this example.

In the exercises you can always see the solution on the next page to compare it with yours.

Decipher the following code:

```
1    S  I  A  F  F  Z  V
2    2  1  2  4  1  5  1
3    7  6  2  3  5  1  1
4    9  _  _  _  _  _  _
5    A  _  _  _  _  _  _
6    3  5  1  4  6  7  2

    Original text: (turn the page)
7    _  _  A  _  _  _  _
8    1  2  3  4  5  6  7
```

ABCDEFGHIJKLMNOPQRSTUVWXYZ_ABCDEFGHIJ

The alphabet for counting letters and spaces.

HOW TO USE THIS BOOK

Here are all the steps to solve the example on page 11.

The first thee are detailed, the others are a little shorter.

COLUMN	STEPS
1	2 + 7 = 9 Look for S in the alphabet and add 9 characters to the right. S + 9 = A Write "A" under your calculated sum 9. Now write "A" in the placeholder number 3 of the original text (line 7).
2	1 + 6 = 7 Look for I in the alphabet and add 7 characters to the right. I + 7 = P Write "P" under your calculated sum 7. Now write "P" in the placeholder number 5 of the original text (line 7).
3	2 + 2 = 4 Look for A in the alphabet and add 4 characters to the right. A + 4 = E Write "E" under your calculated sum 4. Now write "E" in the placeholder number 1 of the original text (line 7).
4	4 + 3 = 7 F + 7 = M (placeholder 4 of the original text)

COLUMN	STEPS
5	1 + 5 = 6 F + 6 = L (placeholder 6 of the original text)
6	5 + 1 = 6 Z + 6 = E (placeholder 7 of the original text)
7	1 + 1 = 2 V + 2 = X (placeholder 2 of the original text)

This is the fully solved example:

```
Decipher the following code:

1   S I A F F Z V
2   2 1 2 4 1 5 1
3   7 6 2 3 5 1 1
4   9 7 4 7 6 6 2
5   A P E M L E X
6   3 5 1 4 6 7 2


    Original text: (turn the page)
7   E X A M P L E
8   1 2 3 4 5 6 7
```

I wish you great success in your daily training!

And now ... let's get started!

day 1

WARM UP!

REMEMBER THE OBJECT: globe

9 • 8 = ____	11 + 22 - 4 = ____
13 + 2 = ____	30 - 3 - 8 = ____
9 + 10 = ____	28 - 15 - 9 = ____
15 + 2 = ____	22 + 4 - 3 = ____
2 • 9 = ____	21 - 6 - 13 = ____
12 + 3 = ____	12 + 28 - 25 = ____
5 • 5 = ____	13 + 27 - 10 = ____
3 + 5 = ____	11 + 10 + 7 = ____
2 + 16 = ____	25 + 26 - 21 = ____
9 + 4 = ____	23 - 11 - 11 = ____
7 • 5 = ____	28 - 16 - 4 = ____
4 + 3 = ____	5 + 13 + 4 = ____
19 - 16 = ____	7 + 11 + 10 = ____
7 • 9 = ____	19 + 11 - 3 = ____
10 • 7 = ____	6 + 11 - 10 = ____
2 • 5 = ____	9 + 5 + 16 = ____
5 • 7 = ____	19 + 4 + 6 = ____
19 - 2 = ____	14 - 3 - 3 = ____
4 • 7 = ____	5 + 8 + 8 = ____
16 - 6 = ____	22 + 19 - 14 = ____

Sketch the picture as precisely as possible and memorize the details so that you can draw it again later:

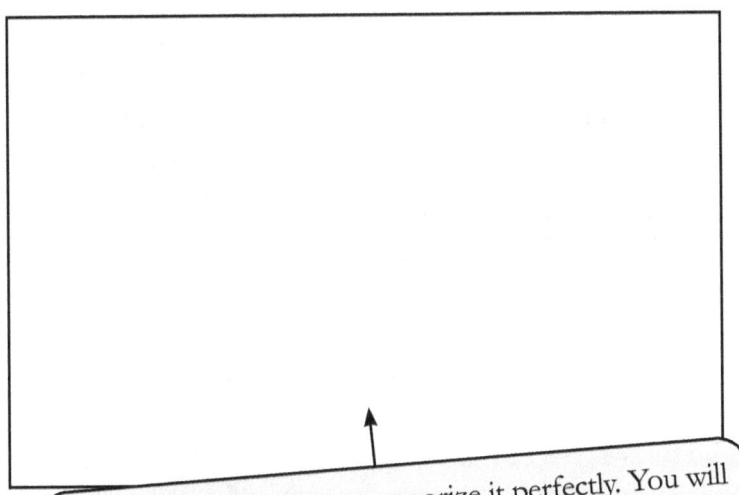

Sketch the image here to memorize it perfectly. You will see: this is much better than just looking at it.

WORDS AND LETTERS

Results for page 16.

You will find an introduction on the pages 10 - 13.

72	29
15	19
19	4
17	23
18	2
15	15
25	30
8	28
18	30
13	1
35	8
7	22
3	28
63	27
70	7
10	30
35	29
17	8
28	21
10	27

Decipher the following code:

```
N K C W
2 4 5 4
3 5 4 5

_ _ _ _

_ _ _ _
4 3 1 2
```

Original text: (turn the page)

```
_ _ _ _
1 2 3 4
```

ABCDEFGHIJKLMNOPQRSTUVWXYZ_ABCDEFGHIJ

Mark and count: MISSISSIPPI

```
PSIMISSISSIPPISSSSIMIIISMISSISSIPPII
ISIIIPSSPSMISSISSIPPIMISIIPPIIISIII
SISISIPPPSMISSISSIPPISMISSISSIPPIIS
PSMISSISSIPPIIMSIISPIPSIMIIISISIISI
SPISSPPIMSIPSIISISPSSISISSSPSSSSISI
ISSIMISSISSIPPISIMISSISSIPPIIISISPI
IIMISSISSIPPIIMPMIIIIIISMISSISSIPPI
SIPPSSPIMIPPPIIPMSSSIIMISSISSIPPIMI
PIIPISSSSPISSSSSSPISIISSPIPSPSSIMII
SMISSISSIPPISIMISSISSIPPISSSISIPMIMI
MISSISSIPPIPSMISSISSIPPIISISPIPMISI
SSIMISPPIPSSIISIMMMIMISSISSIPPIMSPSI
SIMISSISSIPPIPMSSPISPIPPSSSISIISSSI
```

Do it line by line!

Results for
page 21.

Mark and count: ENGLAND

6	14
15	30
18	13
14	35
26	1
24	48
30	38
26	12
54	39
0	28
26	18
12	44
22	29
12	36
70	35
24	4
24	8
11	26
25	7
0	2

```
QFFDJENGLANDENGLANDJXVOHYRJEAMYKLJU
CMZHHKENGLANDJYXEIODENGLANDXEYGFDOB
YVRCHEWAZFFSTDZKFQPQVLSENGLANDECLBO
ZENGLANDSYPVPXPNLKWUCAVNVWAZIALMYWF
WOMRHIMMLQXBYUGEVKPWQIQPZVNZCOEPHBQ
KAYYQPWHFUUYPGVFNNQAZEKFWWDVHUCZPGZ
GCBWENGLANDBNLCILJLKGNPXDNTMVHDNJUH
JXKFJJENGLANDAMWLHGWHPUWRYVCHHAHALI
OMTLFPUOENGLANDKIJDTEADAOENGLANDZPF
URUFNTYGOLHTJIEZXXFQGBHEJXSDAYLVJOO
LENGLANDKMGALWZLMDBFLRIRJXOQPOHHJBR
CCIOGTQWENGLANDENGLANDFQDMRENGLANDN
NPOVKNMZCWYRIOQYZVBVBSENGLANDITMWYK
XENGLANDOPXAKOJOFHYYPZUZYVEVMUOBMRH
AXZRXVVKVBUNMGIQNZVRVENGLANDWIBEQVH
ENGLANDWENGLANDVPZHPENGLANDTKFLMCJR
CSTRKYUQYHENGLANDHXGDAVFENGLANDYAFP
QIVPBLJSDHWTYGZIIDETDBENUKXWSSWDPBR
LOCHBENGLANDFACMQHINGLXXRIMTSGYPPHF
ENGLANDHZHRWENGLANDQAFAQIRWCUKYTAJD
FVETHENGLANDCMGSBMMENGLANDMJYGQQJQC
OAQIOLSKSENGLANDEMRBZENGLANDOHOMPLZ
ENGLANDQYVAEWPYNJLWDEQAXVWTKPQCGCRB
WJWQIHRBQNHFFUENGLANDQKZJYYBIKWTFIU
FXAMENGLANDULPVJZGJLCDQFAVAMPBOBUKK
YDDLKGBFCNRENGLANDPCMHAOEINULYUYFQB
ENGLANDXNCENGLANDKZILXNAMZAWENGLAND
ACCJLDBDWGIHRIGURVENGLANDAFTENGLAND
FZBKSOSGHDHFLXALOBENGLANDKIITDUWGGI
```

Are you sure? See page 194.
Copy the decrypted text on page 197.

CALCULATE

REMEMBER THE ACTIVITY: sailing

4 • 8 = ____	4 • 9 + 60 = ____
38 - 19 = ____	31 + 37 - 39 = ____
36 - 21 = ____	24 + 9 - 9 = ____
7 • 4 = ____	51 + 12 + 31 = ____
14 + 17 = ____	10 • 8 - 11 = ____
23 + 29 = ____	2 • 6 + 7 = ____
28 + 16 = ____	9 + 21 + 24 = ____
11 - 5 = ____	10 • 7 + 13 = ____
27 - 11 = ____	6 • 6 + 42 = ____
38 - 16 = ____	8 • 8 - 42 = ____
24 - 24 = ____	9 • 6 - 43 = ____
18 - 13 = ____	37 - 4 - 17 = ____
21 + 12 = ____	5 • 10 + 21 = ____
24 - 5 = ____	7 • 7 + 42 = ____
38 - 28 = ____	9 • 9 - 23 = ____
37 - 37 = ____	7 • 3 + 39 = ____
7 + 24 = ____	9 + 52 + 6 = ____
39 - 29 = ____	36 - 25 - 8 = ____
25 - 8 = ____	33 - 18 - 11 = ____
16 + 13 = ____	10 • 7 - 34 = ____

Additional tasks - only for math lovers!

2 • 3 = ____	28 - 11 - 3 = ____
9 + 6 = ____	11 + 23 - 4 = ____
6 • 3 = ____	25 + 10 - 22 = ____
21 - 7 = ____	3 • 9 + 8 = ____
9 + 17 = ____	29 - 23 - 5 = ____
13 + 11 = ____	14 + 12 + 22 = ____
18 + 12 = ____	18 + 5 + 15 = ____
6 + 20 = ____	22 + 18 - 28 = ____
6 • 9 = ____	13 + 20 + 6 = ____
5 - 5 = ____	4 • 5 + 8 = ____
21 + 5 = ____	9 + 21 - 12 = ____
5 + 7 = ____	6 • 8 - 4 = ____
9 + 13 = ____	15 + 10 + 4 = ____
18 - 6 = ____	25 + 19 - 8 = ____
7 • 10 = ____	4 • 3 + 23 = ____
5 + 19 = ____	21 - 5 - 12 = ____
8 • 3 = ____	19 - 8 - 3 = ____
28 - 17 = ____	6 • 9 - 28 = ____
7 + 18 = ____	29 - 9 - 13 = ____
29 - 29 = ____	27 - 15 - 10 = ____

Decrypted original text from the previous page:
LET´S

FIND THE NUMBERS!

Do it line by line!

32	96
19	29
15	24
28	94
31	69
52	19
44	54
6	83
16	78
22	22
0	11
5	16
33	71
19	91
10	58
0	60
31	67
10	3
17	4
29	36

Mark and count: 22

```
78999339482247456087383549386
44228158643160738811526238128
21969611479477285290964827632
96597947383796396539897198537
81739220814642454150959657070
98346288981979424422909693775
27935654399412682252090328578
52994051746198332219869228177
92477880381773443022179533020
70397247246512637817683939237
64601831187977631188749912302
79398545504822215227172744457
79988684266243374564546316518
```

Mark and count: 519

```
5192624403053656593589231696
3651409876575915196737452835
3817628055567232776154899145
5086626745941671263977219169
1419907018704239262186411519
6986376478259591296752599608
5191983026347059145193489627
9154296782835198309868435867
5194695495575396003633642311
12061320851959258262155267564
6945856044994891711673441055
6659691835804333108599375512
5102966226444894376082865629
```

Are you sure? See page 195!

Now draw the visualized picture again with as many details as possible:

TRY TO REMEMBER!

What should you find?

- River: _____
- Country: _____
- Decrypted text: _____

What words should you memorize?

- Object: _____
- Activity: _____

day 2

WARM UP!

REMEMBER THE OBJECT: lamp

$12 + 4 =$ ____	$29 - 16 - 8 =$ ____
$9 \cdot 3 =$ ____	$11 + 13 - 4 =$ ____
$4 \cdot 6 =$ ____	$8 + 4 + 8 =$ ____
$4 + 10 =$ ____	$4 + 15 + 9 =$ ____
$8 \cdot 2 =$ ____	$23 - 8 - 8 =$ ____
$14 - 12 =$ ____	$24 - 8 - 15 =$ ____
$3 + 10 =$ ____	$5 + 19 - 4 =$ ____
$4 \cdot 5 =$ ____	$12 + 10 + 8 =$ ____
$18 - 17 =$ ____	$17 + 11 - 18 =$ ____
$3 \cdot 5 =$ ____	$15 - 6 - 6 =$ ____
$9 + 2 =$ ____	$24 + 25 - 25 =$ ____
$10 + 6 =$ ____	$4 + 16 - 17 =$ ____
$19 - 15 =$ ____	$22 - 3 - 14 =$ ____
$12 + 7 =$ ____	$16 - 4 - 8 =$ ____
$8 - 6 =$ ____	$5 + 11 + 9 =$ ____
$14 + 6 =$ ____	$18 - 12 - 3 =$ ____
$14 + 5 =$ ____	$10 + 7 - 10 =$ ____
$4 \cdot 2 =$ ____	$27 - 9 - 9 =$ ____
$2 \cdot 7 =$ ____	$19 + 19 - 27 =$ ____
$2 \cdot 9 =$ ____	$19 + 15 - 29 =$ ____

Sketch the picture as precisely as possible and memorize the details so that you can draw it again later:

WORDS AND LETTERS

16	5
27	20
24	20
14	28
16	7
2	1
13	20
20	30
1	10
15	3
11	24
16	3
4	5
19	4
2	25
20	3
19	7
8	9
14	11
18	5

Decipher the following code:

```
R  Q  B  K  L  _  O  U  N  P
5  1  5  4  3  2  2  2  2  3
4  2  2  4  5  6  1  5  4  4

–  –  –  –  –  –  –  –  –  –
–  –  –  –  –  –  –  –  –  –
6  9  8  1  5  10 4  3  2  7

Original text: (turn the page)
–  –  –  –  –  –  –  –  –  –
1  2  3  4  5  6  7  8  9  10

ABCDEFGHIJKLMNOPQRSTUVWXYZ_ABCDEFGHIJ
```

Mark and count: COLORADO

```
OROCLLOODOCOLORADOCRCDOAOOAOACORLOO
ROROCOAAAOOLODOLAOODLCOLORADODRDAOO
OLROCROADLLOOLCAODROOLLADCACCOOLALC
ROLAORCOLORADOCAOAARCAARDOLRLLODOCL
ROOARLOOODDLLOLOOROADOOCOLORADODLDR
CAADOLDOOCOOROLODLOCDADAARAOOCOOOOO
OOOOCCAACLORAOLCOLAROCOLORADOOCALLO
COCOLORADOOCOOOCOADCDOOARRLRLARDOCR
OOCOLORADOAODCOLORADOOCLCODADOOROOO
CCDDOAOACALDAOCOLORADOCOLLLCOLORADO
ROCAACCOOCOLORADOOOODOROAAOACOORORDO
AOCOLORADOODACOLORADOARDLRRLCOOAOAD
AOROLCLROOAOOROAORDCCORORCCLDDAOORO
```

28

Mark and count: FRANCE

```
ALIRIFRANCEDGHLLRLDHODTCJEXONJPTTEL
PRHBNNFRANCEBCOWCEMZIQMKXTSJFUVENBS
YJTFITUHFRANCEQDFUBGAFYSHUSTSVAVCVY
JSOSOFJEINLTSZJGWZOGUABDBNJPUYUKJKN
WDCWWWFYGOFRANCEDFRANCEYLFHRGABAEKI
XUONIEDOQLIBXLIVGGJGFMLCPHABRFRANCE
VKNFRANCEAGQYMQNCZFRANCEDSTNGQZRBAJ
KZBILGKRSFUULBSCXFQSGWCVVGGOAHNMPFU
VQWWKTNSFLHHCWVZOZQBCKCUFWZYNEPOJZG
EHWOQFBWLJSIQLGHEZEGFRANCETIIMZZQGK
NRWPBNDCWIHEAXLHVFPXZGDRIWXLTJYNXJT
BFRANCEDIIRFTIMOIPRKXMNFRANCEZICAXV
PBRWXIUFCUCGINFRANCELXAFRANCEZCNCIX
DHAMAZYNOVXCDFRANCEGFNNTQXCXMFJPWYZ
DMCZTSGNBAVQZEULPYSXMDRBSGJGFJQIAUE
IXSKXXWQOEHAQZRGUXUZQMIHJXRXBCCCIHV
NTCKWIWFFUFRANCEEOJHFRANCENIHFTKFCY
QFRANCEGAZHYNRBNGLDUEIOAHCMRUFRANCE
MWNEANSCCSBLBMIRFRANCEOHKBZJFRANCEK
BLYULSMUIAWDORFBOFRANCEVYFRANCENURQ
DRDCCKFRANCEFRANCEMQBFRANCEWFRANCEL
LOFRANCEJZBECDJPLVCZTHPFRANCEQJLMQW
FRANCETRDJNJOXGQYSIFRANCEAXDFRANCEB
CUCBESFRANCEGNJXXWSVOTCIQCRLHCPLBMI
QGZKNCVGEBKFRANCESFRANCEXFRANCEKCSV
CKSXLGCRFRANCEKGOFRANCEUNTWUURUVYOX
LTBONWGFRANCEDZUDGTLTFMKZKJBVMNKESO
FRANCETKNWSBWETWAONMYTWXCKTSZFRANCE
ZYJLJKNAXZKEFRANCEHFKMLUUHFRANCETKU
```

40	46
28	48
20	41
6	45
27	2
20	32
10	47
26	14
17	33
10	0
35	37
27	2
29	31
29	1
11	0
30	11
5	34
30	7
0	12
19	35

Are you sure? See page 194.
Copy the decrypted text on page 197.

CALCULATE

REMEMBER THE ACTIVITY: tennis

$7 \cdot 8 =$ ____ $60 + 18 - 22 =$ ____

$3 \cdot 7 =$ ____ $58 + 49 - 29 =$ ____

$9 \cdot 6 =$ ____ $4 \cdot 9 + 42 =$ ____

$19 + 15 =$ ____ $58 - 10 - 11 =$ ____

$22 - 7 =$ ____ $8 \cdot 10 - 22 =$ ____

$13 + 10 =$ ____ $5 \cdot 9 + 50 =$ ____

$8 \cdot 7 =$ ____ $32 + 44 - 46 =$ ____

$19 - 17 =$ ____ $7 \cdot 7 - 26 =$ ____

$30 - 14 =$ ____ $9 \cdot 10 - 40 =$ ____

$26 + 9 =$ ____ $8 + 38 + 46 =$ ____

$6 \cdot 3 =$ ____ $2 \cdot 4 + 36 =$ ____

$7 \cdot 5 =$ ____ $4 \cdot 10 - 29 =$ ____

$30 + 10 =$ ____ $29 + 15 + 31 =$ ____

$6 + 20 =$ ____ $3 \cdot 4 + 24 =$ ____

$18 + 14 =$ ____ $21 + 32 + 16 =$ ____

$19 + 30 =$ ____ $7 \cdot 2 - 5 =$ ____

$20 + 30 =$ ____ $9 \cdot 2 - 14 =$ ____

$10 \cdot 2 =$ ____ $2 \cdot 7 + 56 =$ ____

$18 + 25 =$ ____ $41 + 54 - 39 =$ ____

$7 \cdot 3 =$ ____ $33 + 26 - 7 =$ ____

Additional tasks - only for math lovers!

8 • 5 = ____   5 • 10 - 4 = ____
14 + 14 = ____   22 + 6 + 20 = ____
5 • 4 = ____   2 • 8 + 25 = ____
26 - 20 = ____   2 • 9 + 27 = ____
9 • 3 = ____   30 - 23 - 5 = ____
15 + 5 = ____   20 + 17 - 5 = ____
5 • 2 = ____   23 + 27 - 3 = ____
5 + 21 = ____   5 • 7 - 21 = ____
8 + 9 = ____   15 + 7 + 11 = ____
23 - 13 = ____   23 - 6 - 17 = ____
5 • 7 = ____   21 + 11 + 5 = ____
8 + 19 = ____   18 - 7 - 9 = ____
12 + 17 = ____   21 + 13 - 3 = ____
6 + 23 = ____   11 - 7 - 3 = ____
14 - 3 = ____   18 + 7 - 25 = ____
25 + 5 = ____   12 + 15 - 16 = ____
21 - 16 = ____   11 + 28 - 5 = ____
17 + 13 = ____   22 - 5 - 10 = ____
22 - 22 = ____   3 • 6 - 6 = ____
10 + 9 = ____   4 • 10 - 5 = ____

Decrypted original text from the previous page:
START WITH

31

FIND THE NUMBERS!

56	56
21	78
54	78
34	37
15	58
23	95
56	30
2	23
16	50
35	92
18	44
35	11
40	75
26	36
32	69
49	9
50	4
20	70
43	56
21	52

Mark and count: 43

```
51754588641428986825319519468 4
73881659149334921998255195515 0
72886641217955796543741170771 2
48908743843042345615221346819 6
61775121259578615462968069507 0
60332970874749115120487776654 2
70873543425184664369719591584 3
75483757265970582435124173415 7
85299496732671107337673282786 2
30292813287891121139666491291 5
79847746598192521411789663883 1
43845470297999277278476303530
30869573164621497589259958142 7
```

Mark and count: 523

```
39284873524679682583584452096 2
47552367582689522468538775479 0
43882521052332332218210066076 6
51394147636924266328926917761 1
15822416252335165061763481273 1
88146046756551185941281691631 2
99696661262279381689117962132 0
49580637214678216659835690270 4
47773736870143438734114086941 0
98352337739317637253461932227 6
26392691440116334963539442237 7
52386277664455523646126666952 3
17611018441445760346198152378 9
```

Are you sure? See page 195!

Now draw the visualized picture again with as many details as possible:

TRY TO REMEMBER!

What should you find?

- River: _____
- Country: _____
- Decrypted text: _____

What words should you memorize?

- Object: _____
- Activity: _____

day 3

WARM UP!

REMEMBER THE OBJECT: skateboard

15 - 12 = ____	7 + 27 - 28 = ____
10 • 8 = ____	19 + 5 + 6 = ____
10 • 3 = ____	13 + 13 - 16 = ____
18 - 14 = ____	4 + 15 + 5 = ____
6 • 3 = ____	24 - 11 - 13 = ____
5 + 14 = ____	25 - 9 - 12 = ____
20 - 9 = ____	28 - 17 - 5 = ____
17 + 3 = ____	27 - 9 - 11 = ____
2 • 5 = ____	9 - 3 - 4 = ____
2 • 8 = ____	11 + 8 + 11 = ____
9 + 11 = ____	27 - 11 - 16 = ____
17 - 14 = ____	21 - 10 - 6 = ____
11 + 7 = ____	5 + 19 + 5 = ____
13 - 10 = ____	18 - 9 - 8 = ____
4 - 3 = ____	16 + 16 - 21 = ____
7 • 7 = ____	11 + 11 + 8 = ____
8 + 8 = ____	22 - 10 - 6 = ____
2 + 9 = ____	11 + 5 + 8 = ____
20 - 2 = ____	4 + 12 + 8 = ____
5 - 3 = ____	22 + 20 - 23 = ____

Sketch the picture as precisely as possible and memorize the details so that you can draw it again later:

3	6
80	30
30	10
4	24
18	0
19	4
11	6
20	7
10	2
16	30
20	0
3	5
18	29
3	1
1	11
49	30
16	6
11	24
18	24
2	19

```
Decipher the following code:

F  J  F  S  _  S  L  W  A
1  2  5  4  4  6  6  4  1
1  2  1  5  2  2  2  5  7

—  —  —  —  —  —  —  —  —
—  —  —  —  —  —  —  —  —
2  7  9  8  5  4  1  3  6

Original text: (turn the page)
```

Original text: (turn the page)

```
—  —  —  —  —  —  —  —  —
1  2  3  4  5  6  7  8  9

ABCDEFGHIJKLMNOPQRSTUVWXYZ_ABCDEFGHIJ
```

Mark and count: AMAZON

```
ZMMMAAAOMAMMAAZAAAMAZONNZMONAMAMZAA
OOOAAAZAOAMAZONAAAMAZONAMMOMMNAOOAAZ
NNAAMAZONAMAZONZONMNMAAOMMZAMAZONAZ
OAANNZAMMAMAZONNAMZAMZZAAZMMNMNOZON
OZNOAZNZAONMAAAMAZONAAZNAZAMAZONOAM
OAOAMAZONMAAMAZONZAAMAZONAMNZAAZMZM
OZAMNAMAZZAAAZAZANAMONAAOAOZOAMNOAO
AZMOAMZAMAZONOAAAAMAZAAOAAMAZONOAAM
MANMAMANNZZAMAZONOZNAMAZANNMZOZAMZN
ANNZNNNNONONZANAAOZAAMAZONAAMAANMMA
ANNMAMAZONNAMAZONANAMAMAOZMANZMMAOO
NAZNMZMNAAANNOAOAMZOZAAZZAZAMAZONMN
ZNNZAONOAMAMAZONNMOAOAMAANANZAAOAAM
```

38

Mark and count: GERMANY

	48	50
KBXZEBLVCMGERMANYDMUYXPGERMANYPEACI	15	12
FZQNAYQTGERMANYBDBQYHWPWYKWYEVKQOXR	15	8
QOPUPSYGERMANYCTBCDMGERMANYNQLCWHSW		
TXHNMHQJWTSLDETRJBNXDSSHXESZOOYFWDS	12	17
BFFNPYXWCUKGMMVZRUGERMANYYZJUAUKIAN	27	9
ZKPZYXYLIMTGERMANYESZCCKSPXGERMANYO		
HBIECOTDBRVXNAHOHVZHNLGERMANYYOHQLG	8	1
BZACPSNLNRQZLZKHVGERMANYGERMANYBGNW	29	20
JJHCUJKUXGBESSYNGERMANYLZIOEQRIZGWF		
AFFFDQHESGERMANYSFSHGCAGERMANYOLBOS	64	48
DGTWNOZAGERMANYLEJJWAWPZREKZQOIRRTH	25	46
XNCZGFGEYVCGLZMQHGERMANYWYERQWZQPFM		
CJVGERMANYYOCVGERMANYNGERMANYSTPHXI	36	3
ZFUEGERMANYISSNYYURNGFSJMNFPFUOMKWC	18	9
VGERMANYSJMRIZEJLQNNYTPIZDTNTWYOAXQ		
JMTHGWXGFNFRAMWPGERMANYBIIGAGERMANY	25	30
BTZQSGERMANYDGCMOYKRRTRUOMNOETUIXDB	25	19
ZWXTJDVYOGGERMANYNNNJDXUMRJOVLOULFK		
ECXCGERMANYYMJAADDRHIWINSNAUPCJZCNM	23	13
TVREKOSAOKTASADXFUDRYNGKXOTOGKYKGNU	28	7
QIETGKXGERMANYXKQQGERMANYGODUIQCDIC		
IGDDWXPESQCCQUNKTFWMTLEOBREHWGCKAUR	17	36
XHFXCABQGERMANYDAESFNSUBGDNGERMANYD	30	33
PBUGERMANYFKBCUKGVUTSJRGERMANYGOPXX		
QTWRFBZLVODGFAXAXCGWVJZBALIMCTCFWUZ	17	13
AUUSEBSALNMDEJDVAOEDSPWEYLFLWBZFBAF	4	11
QIODNKJKDBNVOXTWBAGRNGZIACGFAWFHPKX		
GUIAVVRWIMGERMANYVILWPQLKXTABAGVPFZ	27	25
HKOTTIVLGERMANYEAXCMMKUYMTUKHUYSYVC		

Are you sure? See page 194.
Copy the decrypted text on page 197.

CALCULATE

REMEMBER THE ACTIVITY: soccer

8 • 9 = ____	59 + 24 - 38 = ____
9 • 6 = ____	4 • 5 + 49 = ____
39 - 18 = ____	9 • 2 + 53 = ____
30 + 26 = ____	40 - 4 - 25 = ____
28 + 17 = ____	35 + 9 + 35 = ____
7 + 19 = ____	7 • 9 - 52 = ____
22 + 7 = ____	38 + 17 - 39 = ____
34 - 18 = ____	3 • 3 + 16 = ____
10 • 7 = ____	44 + 8 - 35 = ____
10 + 26 = ____	32 + 54 + 11 = ____
17 + 27 = ____	33 + 22 - 42 = ____
39 - 36 = ____	8 • 3 + 60 = ____
9 • 5 = ____	20 + 19 + 27 = ____
6 • 5 = ____	5 • 10 - 43 = ____
33 - 18 = ____	31 + 33 + 19 = ____
3 • 7 = ____	4 • 7 + 14 = ____
17 + 20 = ____	8 + 40 + 51 = ____
33 - 20 = ____	22 + 32 - 15 = ____
16 + 15 = ____	37 + 44 - 8 = ____
6 • 8 = ____	26 - 11 - 11 = ____

day 3

Additional tasks - only for math lovers!

$8 \cdot 6 =$ ____

$27 - 12 =$ ____

$5 \cdot 3 =$ ____

$2 \cdot 6 =$ ____

$9 \cdot 3 =$ ____

$22 - 14 =$ ____

$23 + 6 =$ ____

$8 \cdot 8 =$ ____

$9 + 16 =$ ____

$4 \cdot 9 =$ ____

$5 + 13 =$ ____

$30 - 5 =$ ____

$10 + 15 =$ ____

$18 + 5 =$ ____

$12 + 16 =$ ____

$7 + 10 =$ ____

$3 \cdot 10 =$ ____

$9 + 8 =$ ____

$2 \cdot 2 =$ ____

$21 + 6 =$ ____

$28 + 19 + 3 =$ ____

$22 - 6 - 4 =$ ____

$4 \cdot 9 - 28 =$ ____

$10 + 21 - 14 =$ ____

$14 + 17 - 22 =$ ____

$13 - 7 - 5 =$ ____

$2 \cdot 5 + 10 =$ ____

$15 + 8 + 25 =$ ____

$22 + 4 + 20 =$ ____

$28 - 7 - 18 =$ ____

$4 \cdot 3 - 3 =$ ____

$4 \cdot 6 + 6 =$ ____

$9 \cdot 3 - 8 =$ ____

$10 \cdot 4 - 27 =$ ____

$10 \cdot 3 - 23 =$ ____

$5 + 18 + 13 =$ ____

$20 + 28 - 15 =$ ____

$5 + 25 - 17 =$ ____

$30 - 13 - 6 =$ ____

$2 \cdot 2 + 21 =$ ____

Decrypted original text from the previous page:
THE FINAL

41

FIND THE NUMBERS!

72	45
54	69
21	71
56	11
45	79
26	11
29	16
16	25
70	17
36	97
44	13
3	84
45	66
30	7
15	83
21	42
37	99
13	39
31	73
48	4

Mark and count: 26

```
262626371034668949439358742580
318895703292772681467026522826
206326252220167939233213208687
737626102567267670685892273241
792633213347355473905568932684
934455577813263459539721245969
988735623726101926708649608275
755364937867909294161037664184
563343929492503230525979712655
164126392612474494508222382962
816031638880591477673475657926
329825238726805298994868242488
755894408764898266375869266482
```

Mark and count: 118

```
449947215361254419929131336463
102718191822572270225111206162
351955386626102745518812800913
611449689118481587394152708544
345787118675980372118943142131
266595118499762880401559575812
779246648935540342108181662972
741118615118649250642385415752
797986476294514128795685826216
545776724285581998322641174675
542984118118483184150378320731
838634658101762692781572147779
568294887497301506964575575843
```

Are you sure? See page 195!

REMEMBER!

Now draw the visualized picture again with as many details as possible:

TRY TO REMEMBER!

What should you find?

- River: _____
- Country: _____
- Decrypted text: _____

What words should you memorize?

- Object: _____
- Activity: _____

day 4

WARM UP!

REMEMBER THE OBJECT: plane

$3 \cdot 5 =$ _____	$8 + 12 + 10 =$ _____
$8 \cdot 3 =$ _____	$18 - 5 - 4 =$ _____
$12 - 11 =$ _____	$30 - 3 - 5 =$ _____
$17 - 6 =$ _____	$12 + 7 + 8 =$ _____
$6 + 4 =$ _____	$8 + 5 + 12 =$ _____
$10 \cdot 4 =$ _____	$9 + 4 + 5 =$ _____
$17 - 16 =$ _____	$5 + 13 + 4 =$ _____
$6 \cdot 10 =$ _____	$29 - 5 - 15 =$ _____
$3 + 14 =$ _____	$6 + 9 + 5 =$ _____
$4 \cdot 7 =$ _____	$12 + 12 - 24 =$ _____
$8 + 10 =$ _____	$11 + 26 - 24 =$ _____
$14 - 8 =$ _____	$5 + 7 + 14 =$ _____
$19 - 18 =$ _____	$5 + 7 + 9 =$ _____
$18 - 16 =$ _____	$24 + 16 - 12 =$ _____
$10 - 8 =$ _____	$9 + 15 - 23 =$ _____
$13 - 8 =$ _____	$5 + 4 + 4 =$ _____
$2 + 2 =$ _____	$11 - 6 - 3 =$ _____
$12 + 6 =$ _____	$20 - 11 - 5 =$ _____
$17 - 13 =$ _____	$4 + 17 + 9 =$ _____
$20 - 11 =$ _____	$24 - 17 - 6 =$ _____

Sketch the picture as precisely as possible and memorize the details so that you can draw it again later:

WORDS AND LETTERS

15	30
24	9
1	22
11	27
10	25
40	18
1	22
60	9
17	20
28	0
18	13
6	26
1	21
2	28
2	1
5	13
4	2
18	4
4	30
9	1

```
Decipher the following code:

T  E  M  B  D  _  E  N
6  5  5  1  2  3  4  2
2  4  2  6  3  4  5  2

—  —  —  —  —  —  —  —

—  —  —  —  —  —  —  —
3  5  1  4  6  8  7  2

Original text: (turn the page)
```

```
—  —  —  —  —  —  —  —
1  2  3  4  5  6  7  8

ABCDEFGHIJKLMNOPQRSTUVWXYZ_ABCDEFGHIJ
```

Mark and count: THAMES

```
THAMESHAAEETMEESASTMAMEMSTHAMESTTEE
MSAHSMEAAEHATMAMTMEEAATSESEMHAAEEAH
SEESAMTMMAEEMSMMTHAMESTHAMESATHAMES
MMETTHASMTTAMTSHAEMTHMETSTHAMESMAET
TMTMAATHAMESHETHAMESMTHAMESSEMAMAAS
AETSEHHTTAATSTMMATHMTEMEAHTHHHEMSSS
AETATAAEESHMSTEHHEETMTSSSTHAMESASHT
HTHAMESSAHHMHTEMSTMSTMMESTMSMATHSHH
ETMHEMTEAESEEHHSHMMTMHTHAMESHTEAETS
HATAEEMTTTHAMESMTHAMESMHMSHSSMEAAMA
SETMTSHTETHAMESHMHTTEASAATHMETHAMES
HEHHSHHHTTHMMSAAATHSSMMMAMAETHAMESS
EMTAAEAESMMSMMEEETHAMESMTSEMAMHMTAH
```

48

Mark and count: POLAND

```
TFQVCARCADXXPOLANDOOINXPYPOLANDMNNZ
TNIBBXTIPOLANDASSINXJOPOLANDKMORWBL
TDUWQCAOPOLANDFWEWPOLANDNXZALRMSQDI
TRQUVXPOLANDDPYZFWZSPOLANDISPOLANDW
ISZQUNDSGDVTYYPAYFBEXPOLANDZYQVBDUN
DSUNUYZQGSPOLANDPPBNKYAXRMXKDTRSGZX
GOQWQOGPGYZXGQLAFCIIEXGDNSAUPOLANDD
RIUEUBDVYQRGUPOLANDNJXNKCVPOYJVZAPE
BMQPAYVHCUBSPOLANDDRUPOLANDQSPXPQCV
POLANDMSHOKYYVMCTNAAPPOLANDPUQTATIG
HJVPOLANDMZOMPOLANDTZRJYFLKFSGFPZQL
GFCVMYJXVFPOLANDEUGVWWOWDFKKSIIXXDM
YHKVAZAEBANGBSAPOLANDUSVBPETIFLHGNW
OESOPOLANDCCNLFHXHQWQYFWLRJROWALPIW
DNPOLANDYIPOLANDXCJOJIZMSUQOZGZERSE
VFLMCOMMPLSHODZELGXZQLDOZUJKUWOCODJ
NBFDDSPOLANDPYZFVAPOLANDUKGYSCBKSLQ
YUVKLQZPOLANDPYVMHXRNOWPEOITXLLIIOP
GWXNTVRVRJSRLZNPOLANDZPASKTXYGLJBZU
INSXAAMIKOJOWCPOLANDPEWZVCHRNPOLAND
OXRWACCAAWTOKTZJPOLANDPUZPOLANDQXJE
KRGHJXXFTPOLANDNSOPOLANDDLTPIUGBCBS
ZNWVGJSKIKDHDXJTLPOLANDBWPOLANDFEUJ
BHSIBZRGTOXLBPHLBODPOLANDEUEHLOOOSP
KYQAVABNFOMHDPOLANDEMPOLANDBETEXBLA
TGLFMDDTNFNFMVXFSYCTLPOLANDHHHVTIXY
OXKUAAZAGZGFLPOLANDAPYUDVIBWKBCHANX
GBVFKBYPOLANDMFHIZRHZGFIUCQNDRAVXDJ
SSDTPOLANDGNHIPOLANDEPOLANDNFMOLPMJ
```

1	13
24	15
17	33
30	3
6	48
8	18
4	3
64	1
4	24
40	5
20	44
30	46
72	37
16	24
40	28
6	29
90	8
27	47
45	0
70	7

Are you sure? See page 194.
Copy the decrypted text on page 197.

CALCULATE

REMEMBER THE ACTIVITY: badminton

16 + 16 = ____	52 + 43 - 58 = ____
7 + 13 = ____	29 - 6 - 15 = ____
21 + 6 = ____	6 + 13 - 9 = ____
24 - 7 = ____	60 - 16 - 18 = ____
11 + 24 = ____	43 - 29 - 14 = ____
23 + 27 = ____	44 + 13 - 46 = ____
17 - 12 = ____	30 - 15 - 11 = ____
6 + 12 = ____	37 + 46 - 47 = ____
4 • 10 = ____	7 • 9 - 55 = ____
8 - 8 = ____	8 • 10 - 37 = ____
7 • 4 = ____	5 • 2 + 10 = ____
22 + 26 = ____	38 - 8 - 24 = ____
22 + 6 = ____	15 + 28 + 38 = ____
12 + 25 = ____	34 - 8 - 19 = ____
2 • 7 = ____	46 + 31 - 57 = ____
27 + 13 = ____	46 + 19 + 26 = ____
17 + 24 = ____	48 - 19 - 21 = ____
23 - 14 = ____	24 + 50 + 12 = ____
16 - 7 = ____	8 • 2 - 5 = ____
29 + 14 = ____	9 • 4 + 12 = ____

Additional tasks - only for math lovers!

12 - 11 = ____	4 • 4 - 3 = ____
8 • 3 = ____	4 • 10 - 25 = ____
21 - 4 = ____	3 • 2 + 27 = ____
15 + 15 = ____	29 - 6 - 20 = ____
28 - 22 = ____	12 + 10 + 26 = ____
26 - 18 = ____	13 + 19 - 14 = ____
9 - 5 = ____	6 • 4 - 21 = ____
8 • 8 = ____	25 - 19 - 5 = ____
30 - 26 = ____	16 + 21 - 13 = ____
5 • 8 = ____	22 - 14 - 3 = ____
10 • 2 = ____	19 + 7 + 18 = ____
6 • 5 = ____	6 • 10 - 14 = ____
8 • 9 = ____	16 + 24 - 3 = ____
4 • 4 = ____	16 + 3 + 5 = ____
10 • 4 = ____	5 • 3 + 13 = ____
3 • 2 = ____	16 + 5 + 8 = ____
9 • 10 = ____	17 + 11 - 20 = ____
9 • 3 = ____	13 + 7 + 27 = ____
9 • 5 = ____	24 - 20 - 4 = ____
7 • 10 = ____	20 - 7 - 6 = ____

Decrypted original text from the previous page:
TRAINING

32	37
20	8
27	10
17	26
35	0
50	11
5	4
18	36
40	8
0	43
28	20
48	6
28	81
37	7
14	20
40	91
41	8
9	86
9	11
43	48

Mark and count: 79

```
977824432079468217932824239598
79752243322343501222747950951 5
11853382588079704282483318591 8
49482086405750117969374594285 0
78448016749374811580777131267 6
27439379797432923035691535832 1
92118272828791548344088214615
79142183814672813866773129995 9
43657866577564792581753282619 8
79953635875119513988854538663 9
63327683422872888376911913361 6
36807923238031595088537779794 1
39649679435219142779991236569 2
```

Mark and count: 277

```
65427168788878527712139027791 8
43889427362164827796391867880 1
44526927774362146127672535472 0
59626911471564257057651410817 4
45180910323031313699138084422 5
30863762622586473080352845274 9
31954715988791527716625125227 7
91672660025716627774995349779 7
63870950244531617819076239810 7
80545347459041540143250627719 8
44814278684459459943283539481 5
95648147041894115860421653541 5
22363314629327778675454327744 6
```

Are you sure? See page 195!

Now draw the visualized picture again with as many details as possible:

```
┌─────────────────────────────────────┐
│                                       │
│                                       │
│                                       │
│                                       │
│                                       │
│                                       │
│                                       │
│                                       │
└─────────────────────────────────────┘
```

TRY TO REMEMBER!

What should you find?

- River: _____
- Country: _____
- Decrypted text: _____

What words should you memorize?

- Object: _____
- Activity: _____

day 5

WARM UP!

REMEMBER THE OBJECT: ball

$6 \cdot 10 =$ ____	$11 + 12 - 18 =$ ____
$2 \cdot 8 =$ ____	$8 + 6 + 13 =$ ____
$10 + 6 =$ ____	$25 + 17 - 21 =$ ____
$4 \cdot 7 =$ ____	$5 + 12 + 13 =$ ____
$18 - 18 =$ ____	$27 + 13 - 30 =$ ____
$20 - 11 =$ ____	$10 + 6 + 6 =$ ____
$6 + 4 =$ ____	$13 + 25 - 15 =$ ____
$5 + 3 =$ ____	$24 + 24 - 18 =$ ____
$3 \cdot 3 =$ ____	$28 - 4 - 21 =$ ____
$10 \cdot 7 =$ ____	$25 - 10 - 11 =$ ____
$10 \cdot 9 =$ ____	$7 + 8 + 6 =$ ____
$8 + 10 =$ ____	$19 + 6 - 10 =$ ____
$2 \cdot 6 =$ ____	$20 + 4 - 22 =$ ____
$8 + 4 =$ ____	$26 + 27 - 26 =$ ____
$18 - 15 =$ ____	$15 + 5 + 8 =$ ____
$16 - 13 =$ ____	$16 + 5 - 21 =$ ____
$6 + 3 =$ ____	$27 + 11 - 25 =$ ____
$10 \cdot 8 =$ ____	$9 + 25 - 17 =$ ____
$4 \cdot 9 =$ ____	$26 + 18 - 17 =$ ____
$7 \cdot 6 =$ ____	$5 + 22 - 12 =$ ____

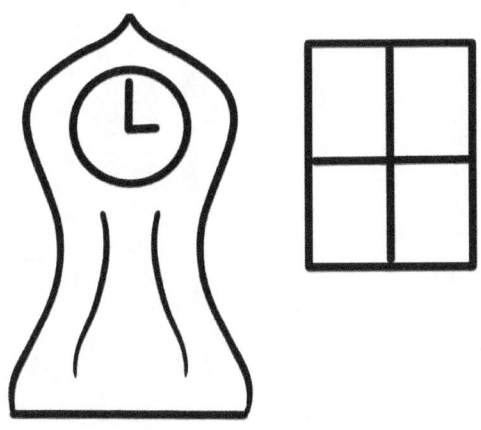

Sketch the picture as precisely as possible and memorize the details so that you can draw it again later:

60	5
16	27
16	21
28	30
0	10
9	22
10	23
8	30
9	3
70	4
90	21
18	15
12	2
12	27
3	28
3	0
9	13
80	17
36	27
42	15

```
Decipher the following code:

P  I  O  S  Z  O  G  G  Y  A  Y  X  T  N
5  7  1  6  2  1  4  5  4  2  6  3  2  4
1  2  2  2  4  3  4  4  2  2  1  5  3  3

-  -  -  -  -  -  -  -  -  -  -  -  -  -

-  -  -  -  -  -  -  -  -  -  -  -  -  -
10 12 6  4  9  8  2  5  14 7  13 11 1  3

Original text: (turn the page)

-  -  -  -  -  -  -  -  -  -  -  -  -  -
1  2  3  4  5  6  7  8  9  10 11 12 13 14

ABCDEFGHIJKLMNOPQRSTUVWXYZ_ABCDEFGHIJ
```

Mark and count: NILE

```
EILNNELNNILELINNINILENNILELNILELIEL
EENEENNLLLENNILELNEENEIINENIELIINIL
ILLLLLNELNILEILLNNLNINIINENNINILENN
ELNILEINLNEINEINIINILELNIIIIEEENENE
INILEELELNEEILIENENELNILEILINILEEEI
LEENNNEEINLINNLENILEIINNEEIIELINLE
NLLNEIEINNNNENIENEILNILEELLELNLNILE
INILEIILILNIILLINEIEIIILIENNLNILEEL
INILEEENEEENEIILNIEENEENLLLIEILLLEL
ILNINELNLEIEENNILELIEIILLLILEELNEII
INELNEEINIEILINLNEIILEINILENLLLEELN
IIINILELLLILNILELLNILEENLINNELLLNE
ILLNILENILELNNIEELIILNNLLEEEENILELL
```

Mark and count: NETHERLANDS

```
RQZCWWUQDWLMQDNLXMTXSTQFIXJNMHNCOYO
ABZBUNWQBUAHWFHONETHERLANDSWVZKNUNG
MWSUBNETHERLANDSCLQXTNETHERLANDSMPV
LBNETHERLANDSQSLOTAMNETHERLANDSVGTN
GANWPZWWIFTRVKCWRBOWJMDSZCYGXUDNEKJ
QUEABSQFTHSFFNETHERLANDSOCUAEBGTJVZ
ZNETHERLANDSDGNETHERLANDSMROZMHUGJR
TAOLAXIKIOWGVNETHERLANDSQNVHUIBJWIF
MKZWUTBNUVCEBUPPOJUQIIPHHERIXZRLAJU
NETHERLANDSYZQRYYAHEUQTFCXELONIRUQK
SFJBCDYONETHERLANDSYSWNETHERLANDSJT
NETHERLANDSRNSAUGOXZQNENETHERLANDSK
JEWAZCYJRTNETHERLANDSTNBOCRIYSPQSXY
SBPQZNETHERLANDSSJCIFVQSHZZXUOJFQHC
NETHERLANDSNETHERLANDSWNRDBBTAPJJUF
OBSVZXAALNETHERLANDSCTPCGXVJWGUEJBU
GFWCTHVZHEJXCNIFYAASFDARNITSFGJXABW
EDJSNETHERLANDSBWNETHERLANDSGTLDTUQ
WLRBNETHERLANDSPDNHKRISKGYKNMDISZFU
XUGYUFQQPHAFPCPLPFDPBWXTMUMZWVTVVEU
YBMLPECEYOIWHAYNETHERLANDSKSMDDUOMY
MIMWKYEZSPNETHERLANDSZOJNYLFQUOKIQE
HMBEETXDHRTZWNETHERLANDSDLHZROWJVEK
AUUUPSHRWCYNETHERLANDSJYPSHRBANRWKA
NKGAUBJWUWFATVJPBUULDTJQKKIYVDEUPWP
VSNCYQBNETHERLANDSFRWNETHERLANDSJSD
APOLCIFTZYRNETHERLANDSAYNWQYNOUZNHQ
GIMOCMGHLZHBLIWHXNETHERLANDSRRZYBEQ
RKOLYHNBDMYZYUFLTJMJCAQYLBWLSOCTWBH
```

64	15
26	19
30	48
18	22
22	1
32	38
36	35
11	2
42	38
6	5
30	44
2	4
48	39
25	7
23	29
24	35
0	26
24	19
11	22
20	43

Are you sure? See page 194.
Copy the decrypted text on page 197.

CALCULATE

REMEMBER THE ACTIVITY: swimming

16 + 18 = _____	53 - 35 - 17 = _____
12 + 10 = _____	8 • 7 + 24 = _____
20 - 5 = _____	8 • 8 - 46 = _____
9 + 11 = _____	8 • 4 + 14 = _____
8 • 9 = _____	44 + 24 + 11 = _____
4 • 5 = _____	16 - 4 - 12 = _____
8 • 5 = _____	43 - 17 - 17 = _____
21 + 19 = _____	60 + 56 - 39 = _____
30 + 10 = _____	7 • 6 - 34 = _____
5 • 3 = _____	48 - 39 - 7 = _____
36 - 5 = _____	3 • 7 + 9 = _____
17 + 6 = _____	4 • 4 + 23 = _____
27 + 28 = _____	56 - 13 - 38 = _____
5 • 2 = _____	6 • 8 + 43 = _____
3 • 5 = _____	17 + 43 - 39 = _____
19 + 28 = _____	19 + 28 - 33 = _____
12 + 15 = _____	6 + 10 + 37 = _____
9 • 7 = _____	43 + 13 - 4 = _____
40 - 30 = _____	5 • 8 - 17 = _____
6 • 5 = _____	2 • 5 + 32 = _____

Additional tasks - only for math lovers!

8 • 8 = ____   28 + 4 - 17 = ____

21 + 5 = ____   9 + 25 - 15 = ____

10 + 20 = ____   28 + 24 - 4 = ____

9 • 2 = ____   3 • 9 - 5 = ____

10 + 12 = ____   16 - 7 - 8 = ____

4 • 8 = ____   12 + 18 + 8 = ____

9 • 4 = ____   17 + 24 - 6 = ____

18 - 7 = ____   9 • 3 - 25 = ____

6 • 7 = ____   7 • 8 - 18 = ____

3 • 2 = ____   21 - 10 - 6 = ____

15 + 15 = ____   8 • 2 + 28 = ____

24 - 22 = ____   4 • 6 - 20 = ____

8 • 6 = ____   15 + 10 + 14 = ____

15 + 10 = ____   25 - 13 - 5 = ____

14 + 9 = ____   13 + 20 - 4 = ____

28 - 4 = ____   10 + 10 + 15 = ____

12 - 12 = ____   3 • 2 + 20 = ____

7 + 17 = ____   16 + 12 - 9 = ____

14 - 3 = ____   19 + 14 - 11 = ____

11 + 9 = ____   3 • 10 + 13 = ____

Decrypted original text from the previous page:
YOU PRESEVERED

FIND THE NUMBERS!

34	1
22	80
15	18
20	46
72	79
20	0
40	9
40	77
40	8
15	2
31	30
23	39
55	5
10	91
15	21
47	14
27	53
63	52
10	23
30	42

Mark and count: 59

```
16282559709753518448 3474598542
60808410789421179045 99766 81360
24571929216675677557 4971835957
65591934115439355438 6273244317
49563499577676443516 8062693320
40553759583437822268 1189145728
40662424457180777045 4729729265
36133611576450593468 3959875787
72354279387575429762 4620273930
91731191241340516256 8628166645
58891483216893835312 1531599991
83495938251836829027 4027739173
84585270356796522096 56676327561
```

Mark and count: 524

```
25169073252412330070 9175755261
18870515264498061160 8836137839
84338869767962840347 52576 65580
52958711746699729830 2567165615
60891656138279872457 8500361268
32825560252438652495 8527860915
53331039850043410756 8875421165
74652487342926456440 2793452347
27852860710652469852 2186388670
38697531467088292930 7211532524
74488127630952452467 7505520600
51137855566731845377 6416420644
98887883215952462264 0767618553
```

Are you sure? See page 195!

Now draw the visualized picture again with as many details as possible:

TRY TO REMEMBER!

What should you find?

- River: _____
- Country: _____
- Decrypted text: _____

What words should you memorize?

- Object: _____
- Activity: _____

day 6

WARM UP!

REMEMBER THE OBJECT: table

6 + 5 = _____	11 + 14 + 5 = _____
15 - 4 = _____	7 + 13 + 10 = _____
20 - 5 = _____	29 - 5 - 21 = _____
12 + 2 = _____	23 - 6 - 17 = _____
7 • 6 = _____	5 + 11 - 4 = _____
5 • 5 = _____	27 + 9 - 15 = _____
20 - 20 = _____	10 + 7 + 13 = _____
2 • 4 = _____	23 - 5 - 5 = _____
6 • 9 = _____	26 - 16 - 3 = _____
5 • 6 = _____	17 + 9 + 4 = _____
5 + 12 = _____	11 + 5 + 13 = _____
10 + 10 = _____	26 - 21 - 3 = _____
3 + 7 = _____	4 + 16 - 8 = _____
13 - 10 = _____	30 - 8 - 15 = _____
6 - 6 = _____	12 + 13 - 7 = _____
11 + 7 = _____	15 + 5 + 5 = _____
16 - 12 = _____	25 + 27 - 22 = _____
9 • 10 = _____	10 + 8 + 12 = _____
2 • 5 = _____	25 - 14 - 8 = _____
7 + 4 = _____	17 + 8 - 12 = _____

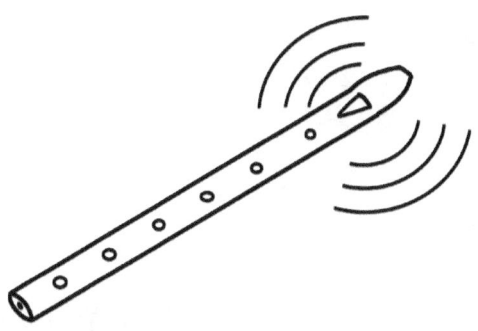

Sketch the picture as precisely as possible and memorize the details so that you can draw it again later:

11	30
11	30
15	3
14	0
42	12
25	21
0	30
8	13
54	7
30	30
17	29
20	2
10	12
3	7
0	18
18	25
4	30
90	30
10	3
11	13

```
Decipher the following code:

Y V I X K Y O A Y
1 6 7 3 2 1 2 7 4
2 2 2 3 3 6 3 1 2
– – – – – – – – –
– – – – – – – – –
3 4 2 7 1 8 5 6 9

Original text: (turn the page)
– – – – – – – – –
1 2 3 4 5 6 7 8 9

ABCDEFGHIJKLMNOPQRSTUVWXYZ_ABCDEFGHIJ
```

Mark and count: VOLGA

```
GLGOLVVOLGAOLLAVOLGAAAVLVOLGAAOVOVG
VOGLOOOVOLGALAVVOLGAVOGGALGOOAGOVGG
LAGAGLGGOOGAVOGVAVAGVAGVOAOOVLLGGAV
LLVVLOOGGVOLVLVVLALGAVGAVVVVLAAAOAL
GLLAALOLOAOOOAOGVGAAAVAAVVOLGALVLVL
OVGGAVVOLGALLGLVOVVOLGAAGGOLAAAOAVV
LOLALVGGGGGGOLVOLGAVVGVOLGAOLAVOLGA
GVOAAALGLVAAVOLGAVOOVOLGALLVOLGAAVV
ALGOVLVVVVVOAOVAALLVLLGLGAOALVOLGAO
ALAALAVVOLGAAAVGGAVAOVVLAOGVAVGGGAV
LOVLGGAAVOLGAGVAVAVLOALGGLLAGOALOOA
LLAGVLVLALAGLALVAVOVLGGVOLGAAGVOLGA
AVVOLGAGAVOLGAAAGVLVAVVALGVLVAAOVLG
```

Mark and count: CUBA

```
BIOGVMAOBIXFJZKWNKXGKDBCRTTTJJWROJB
SRCUBAMZCUBAPIYDEUCUBAQHHGQMCGPVBKZ
ZCUBARAHUJQUQPWALMCFCWICXTORBKCCVNL
ARPUOOJUHGJJVNGEOWCLFHSGLJHVBBZPIWS
TCUBANUXNDNNDXZZQRZTCLHHMLNTLIQCXUS
IAELWCUBANYNNLDLJCUBAVCUBAPUNHYQASO
NHHECUBACPTBNNUEBTCATXXYBGIKZGQOYJJ
GIZECUBAQMCUBATONLPWSEYHVQVQMQPWIDQ
SEYSZODHBYFVYJVBHECUBANQWLZJBKPJGAT
CCUBAPZTLNRGZCCUBAZVIEIPWKVYHHUYBBW
DDVVCUBACUBAURMMSMIZODSDACUBAZTSPDV
GTOGTMEGNDSVOJCUBAPXQDTWGBYCUBAIRHW
ZSCFMAODABHYRVWNKUGMTENRSACUBAUOAPX
CUBAHIVFPZHLDIKOUPUCUBAXCUBANJCDLJA
LYQLMZUJQCUBAOLUUYUIHWKHVACUBAIVOUJ
ZMGREDGZBYACIWPVAZPRBPPRLAJCUBAPXVZ
CUBACUBAPOFGAHCQLPCUBAHONNSACUBAPUA
YYEKOSCVOZOPVIAEWCUBAMCUBAHCUBACUBA
IRTUGTMEOGXDATGBYRGDMPCUBAKLBVQYZAU
FOXHXOLXCUBAMYTCUBABBYRRTAUZBNVCUBA
HVTNGYQGNUJBGPPLYVLRUNPAZWLLZYEWXPT
OLUCDCOJHOXPZCUBALTYVBPXTIFIIXBHOWD
XNFZWCUBASKVGIUQUGQECHLVYVQLZIGIPVU
NMXRJCYZQFFYSUXXRCUBAVGFWXCUBAMDMKC
ZIETEDTYCUBAEWKBNJLUTHUQKNDQJZIKJUT
PCJXXPNTZEQTLJRRGNZYLVBTSKKHWRHPJBS
ZQDTDUMDFCJOYIMSDVFUJRZESZVMRAPANFD
CUBAACUBAVMUMPLOAQPDXEJVMVMFCTKAWYT
PKKVJLFAIEDZMQCZTUYLOCUBARSZYXSBAVK
```

11	37
5	43
30	48
15	36
13	43
24	44
23	12
30	49
16	15
12	9
22	4
17	17
81	6
23	22
16	38
29	50
22	22
30	20
20	1
80	16

Are you sure? See page 194.
Copy the decrypted text on page 197.

CALCULATE

REMEMBER THE ACTIVITY: hiking

$4 \cdot 6 = \underline{\hphantom{00}}$	$30 + 43 - 52 = \underline{\hphantom{00}}$
$6 \cdot 7 = \underline{\hphantom{00}}$	$5 \cdot 4 + 58 = \underline{\hphantom{00}}$
$38 - 18 = \underline{\hphantom{00}}$	$46 - 36 - 5 = \underline{\hphantom{00}}$
$6 \cdot 5 = \underline{\hphantom{00}}$	$41 + 19 - 43 = \underline{\hphantom{00}}$
$5 \cdot 7 = \underline{\hphantom{00}}$	$41 + 37 - 15 = \underline{\hphantom{00}}$
$10 \cdot 4 = \underline{\hphantom{00}}$	$11 + 27 - 23 = \underline{\hphantom{00}}$
$8 \cdot 9 = \underline{\hphantom{00}}$	$58 - 20 - 30 = \underline{\hphantom{00}}$
$17 + 8 = \underline{\hphantom{00}}$	$6 \cdot 8 - 38 = \underline{\hphantom{00}}$
$6 \cdot 8 = \underline{\hphantom{00}}$	$16 + 20 + 14 = \underline{\hphantom{00}}$
$29 - 23 = \underline{\hphantom{00}}$	$15 + 49 + 19 = \underline{\hphantom{00}}$
$29 - 20 = \underline{\hphantom{00}}$	$39 + 34 + 25 = \underline{\hphantom{00}}$
$4 \cdot 4 = \underline{\hphantom{00}}$	$8 \cdot 5 - 16 = \underline{\hphantom{00}}$
$9 \cdot 3 = \underline{\hphantom{00}}$	$4 \cdot 10 + 22 = \underline{\hphantom{00}}$
$25 + 27 = \underline{\hphantom{00}}$	$2 \cdot 6 - 10 = \underline{\hphantom{00}}$
$10 \cdot 7 = \underline{\hphantom{00}}$	$10 \cdot 6 - 43 = \underline{\hphantom{00}}$
$13 + 27 = \underline{\hphantom{00}}$	$9 \cdot 9 - 10 = \underline{\hphantom{00}}$
$7 \cdot 3 = \underline{\hphantom{00}}$	$5 \cdot 7 + 52 = \underline{\hphantom{00}}$
$7 \cdot 5 = \underline{\hphantom{00}}$	$3 \cdot 10 - 6 = \underline{\hphantom{00}}$
$3 \cdot 7 = \underline{\hphantom{00}}$	$17 + 28 + 28 = \underline{\hphantom{00}}$
$12 - 11 = \underline{\hphantom{00}}$	$45 - 32 - 5 = \underline{\hphantom{00}}$

day 6

(Additional tasks - only for math lovers!)

30 - 19 = ____   15 + 26 - 4 = ____

16 - 11 = ____   3 • 9 + 16 = ____

19 + 11 = ____   24 + 15 + 9 = ____

25 - 10 = ____   5 + 25 + 6 = ____

24 - 11 = ____   3 • 5 + 28 = ____

6 + 18 = ____   29 + 4 + 11 = ____

14 + 9 = ____   2 • 3 + 6 = ____

3 • 10 = ____   8 • 3 + 25 = ____

9 + 7 = ____   9 • 4 - 21 = ____

6 • 2 = ____   2 • 2 + 5 = ____

14 + 8 = ____   25 + 7 - 28 = ____

7 + 10 = ____   5 + 25 - 13 = ____

9 • 9 = ____   28 - 16 - 6 = ____

5 + 18 = ____   8 + 28 - 14 = ____

8 • 2 = ____   4 + 18 + 16 = ____

7 + 22 = ____   5 • 6 + 20 = ____

17 + 5 = ____   6 • 8 - 26 = ____

10 • 3 = ____   5 • 9 - 25 = ____

27 - 7 = ____   27 - 22 - 4 = ____

8 • 10 = ____   9 • 5 - 29 = ____

Decrypted original text from the previous page:
PRACTICED

71

FIND THE NUMBERS!

24	21
42	78
20	5
30	17
35	63
40	15
72	8
25	10
48	50
6	83
9	98
16	24
27	62
52	2
70	17
40	71
21	87
35	24
21	73
1	8

Mark and count: 18

```
68658883639055475040681313183534
88628210557818601452894161118 98
78231890766725781820376397 8934
86182639188818874137382718 1763
47438888188571622018494038 8536
18616010204110992633846910 9757
32424770989451185161165259 1979
84858475559633749635345818 1836
48976170962588462297295547 2470
18906321733170149395182868 7859
90681860556311106049741793 1430
91181918179582772262486132 5378
99359096876072232418814533 8278
```

Mark and count: 973

```
18246668026885797322349771 4328
58744085317717655057228251 3429
59297381985975719243697897 3596
11965717197353135621288232 9294
29897092398618791753210280 4834
24137099121382311697377958 6973
82253774754590166671715575 9111
22041183399458753560480928 6197
43226397314718512044239828 2880
87743162779581599691736691 0278
48588486384258894499546191 2921
54047413235314626797368897 3770
12971723616040597343530187 8582
```

72

Are you sure? See page 195!

Now draw the visualized picture again with as many details as possible:

TRY TO REMEMBER!

What should you find?

* River: _____
* Country: _____
* Decrypted text: _____

What words should you memorize?

* Object: _____
* Activity: _____

day 7

WARM UP!

REMEMBER THE OBJECT: camera

5 + 10 = _____	17 + 9 - 5 = _____
2 • 7 = _____	13 + 4 + 9 = _____
2 + 16 = _____	11 + 14 + 4 = _____
2 • 8 = _____	9 + 11 - 3 = _____
7 + 8 = _____	23 - 9 - 8 = _____
10 + 6 = _____	4 + 12 + 4 = _____
13 - 10 = _____	12 + 11 - 14 = _____
3 • 8 = _____	7 + 7 + 11 = _____
7 • 9 = _____	29 - 11 - 9 = _____
2 • 2 = _____	6 + 11 + 5 = _____
4 + 12 = _____	26 + 4 - 25 = _____
5 + 5 = _____	5 + 5 + 14 = _____
3 • 2 = _____	28 - 25 - 3 = _____
11 - 8 = _____	23 + 8 - 4 = _____
6 + 11 = _____	25 + 5 - 23 = _____
15 - 15 = _____	29 - 23 - 3 = _____
16 - 13 = _____	20 - 11 - 4 = _____
4 + 8 = _____	6 + 9 - 13 = _____
9 • 10 = _____	30 - 4 - 10 = _____
10 • 2 = _____	25 + 5 - 6 = _____

Sketch the picture as precisely as possible and memorize the details so that you can draw it again later:

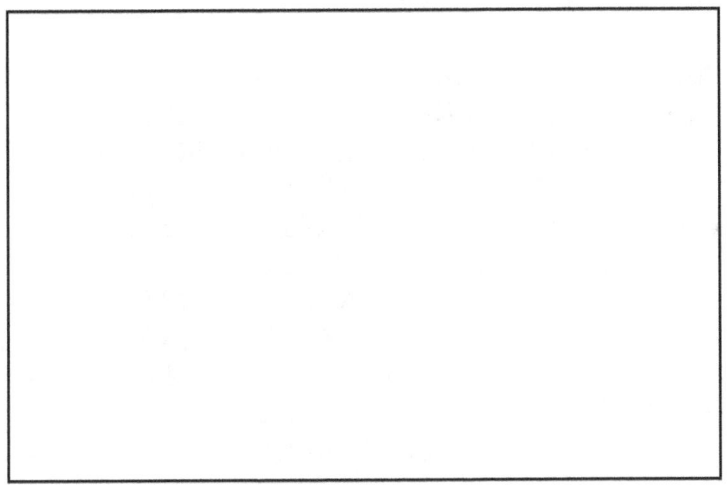

15	21
14	26
18	29
16	17
15	6
16	20
3	9
24	25
63	9
4	22
16	5
10	24
6	0
3	27
17	7
0	3
3	5
12	2
90	16
20	24

Decipher the following code:

```
L H W T U F Z W D
2 2 3 1 4 2 1 3 2
6 5 1 6 3 6 4 2 6

_ _ _ _ _ _ _ _ _
_ _ _ _ _ _ _ _ _
5 4 2 6 7 8 9 1 3
```

Original text: (turn the page)

```
_ _ _ _ _ _ _ _ _
1 2 3 4 5 6 7 8 9
```

ABCDEFGHIJKLMNOPQRSTUVWXYZ_ABCDEFGHIJ

Mark and count: LENA

```
NLENAAAEELENALLEALLALLEEENALENAEAEE
NELLELENALANEEAALENALLEEEANENNENANN
AALENALELENAAAENAALNLENALNEANLAEALA
AEAAELAELEEEENELEANEEELLNANEELLLNLA
AAAELANNLELENAENNLELENANANNAANALLLA
ELNNALLNEALELLEENLENALNALEEEEAAELEA
NELLEAEENANNLANLENANELEELALEEANANNN
AEEANEELLLENALLEALNNLELAEELENANEELA
AENLLEELALELENANAANAEAANLENAAAEENAL
ALLENAANLENAANNANLLAENLNELENALNALEE
NELENAALEAEEENEAALENNLANAELENALENAA
ALEALEANENALALNAANAALLEAENAANAEALAL
LENELENNEAEENNEANALAEENLLELLLLNALLN
```

Mark and count: CANADA

```
HOYAPQGLENCANADAHIFTCANADARHYRZQOJY
CQXPTLICRCANADAKSZLJECANADAKTQRSPUV
BMCWNRMGPLLRWFMFUWZCANADAYCANADAATP
CANADAMJNKKTOCANADAYMYXSYLAFYOHDEUI
TUJCANADAQKHFTARMDQNMGHAOCRMOPYAJNB
GWKZQXQTJJECANADASRCPOOTXFLNGFLNWHQ
IXCSCANADAPLXPBGSTQCANADABPFWWRTZMN
ZCANADACEOYHPHMYJBVVCAUFOZEPDHHPMVO
NVCESJXLJCCANADAVHBCANADAXCCANADAOG
VOMERCANADAKSYWNAHGRCXDUSKOFHEDGFGX
CANADABMCANADAOJDECHZVJXKQFNXCJURFP
OORGCANADACJRKNDAIWJYDSECANADAXFFOA
WSCBIUZSQRLCANADACANADALTZXQKKXEJOG
WIACANADAFTKBQXBIVHKRBFERDYCANADACX
ZZREPFQHLXWXWWYVBXKBLFCANADAJVXXGDK
YFNOSGELLVCANADAOCANADANGHHSKAPSRNZ
HTUFAFGZAATRDVKJCANADAJUMQTCSBNXSMV
OYDWBEIQGMNBOHKQQVXOZGVJDFAFJUXZMKS
KIJMWHOCFJFHDGVPXCANADALSYKALAVPJEF
WOCANADALTRLNOPGQIKDNXCANADAFNTSUBO
CANADAPJISFPFGUCANADAUOQCUBZMMNGHDN
TNKACEAPJTKJUGKEACANADAZGRXKWRNSSUH
CFJUHDUIWTCANADAHWXIKBJSEEQKOIKIVOF
BJLBOQULERWUIAKJKRDZCIHNYMJLCNFRUBW
QLWBPVHSHLINHWLCANADAZPBCANADAMOTUZ
SWVHWMWZVYIUGCANADAWICLQMZUWECANADA
XOZVMDSYSELLMLCANADADSACDQMFRHCLUHK
WOLQHQUCANADAPOADDHVKDWVBTICANADAWT
VKCANADACJNXHGDCANADACOPOWJHZTNPTJV
```

2	43
18	9
28	10
9	21
29	48
32	42
4	25
40	17
7	2
16	20
50	3
6	33
5	26
20	49
28	45
24	2
2	31
10	50
50	8
27	33

Are you sure? See page 194.
Copy the decrypted text on page 197.

CALCULATE

REMEMBER THE ACTIVITY: rowing

6 • 6 = _____	15 + 58 + 13 = _____
33 - 24 = _____	4 • 6 + 57 = _____
5 • 8 = _____	5 • 6 + 37 = _____
20 + 26 = _____	4 • 8 - 32 = _____
25 + 10 = _____	3 • 9 + 48 = _____
10 + 29 = _____	6 • 5 + 47 = _____
39 - 29 = _____	15 + 27 + 52 = _____
13 - 6 = _____	7 • 6 - 39 = _____
32 - 5 = _____	4 • 5 - 4 = _____
9 • 9 = _____	10 + 22 + 12 = _____
40 - 33 = _____	8 • 3 + 23 = _____
4 • 4 = _____	7 • 8 - 44 = _____
22 + 23 = _____	7 • 6 - 42 = _____
28 + 13 = _____	10 • 3 + 9 = _____
22 + 20 = _____	51 - 9 - 23 = _____
14 + 15 = _____	5 • 7 + 53 = _____
3 • 5 = _____	44 - 12 - 31 = _____
3 • 3 = _____	54 + 52 - 46 = _____
9 • 3 = _____	7 + 44 + 12 = _____
18 + 10 = _____	43 - 4 - 20 = _____

day 7

Additional tasks - only for math lovers!

22 - 20 = ____

6 • 3 = ____

7 • 4 = ____

26 - 17 = ____

24 + 5 = ____

4 • 8 = ____

2 • 2 = ____

8 • 5 = ____

19 - 12 = ____

8 + 8 = ____

10 • 5 = ____

28 - 22 = ____

24 - 19 = ____

10 + 10 = ____

22 + 6 = ____

6 • 4 = ____

12 - 10 = ____

17 - 7 = ____

5 • 10 = ____

9 + 18 = ____

8 • 9 - 29 = ____

8 • 3 - 15 = ____

2 • 9 - 8 = ____

6 + 23 - 8 = ____

18 + 15 + 15 = ____

28 + 22 - 8 = ____

8 • 5 - 15 = ____

5 + 20 - 8 = ____

25 - 10 - 13 = ____

21 + 20 - 21 = ____

20 - 8 - 9 = ____

19 + 10 + 4 = ____

11 + 18 - 3 = ____

10 + 19 + 20 = ____

4 • 5 + 25 = ____

12 + 13 - 23 = ____

13 + 11 + 7 = ____

11 + 13 + 26 = ____

8 + 24 - 24 = ____

4 + 26 + 3 = ____

Decrypted original text from the previous page:
A LOT AND

FIND THE NUMBERS!

36	86
9	81
40	67
46	0
35	75
39	77
10	94
7	3
27	16
81	44
7	47
16	12
45	0
41	39
42	19
29	88
15	1
9	60
27	63
28	19

Mark and count: 69

14224593247672932264944632931036193251626962559926528470922396443832957038608484461379692469899555896991101487669069951094378592608565787769697514371066728293662129131440398521696989381588284894691346201121396237442041941834247168108739162671647154489412838014323414805839588163411437837486671491282291236969984489141111813528298758696183968992691442954056923670872082392627163696506639834842424150385706860330450523475565638875203743723203937697463453951438894975634471356723223141723982639914298156816723487373280723657142894630589909127628792880855541197500566756446812118938600723723140723878393135778987634723749654179723723397809437637660121536650326359855723709491723358939723135558810103452559616797327908415612116304406725723463888581611621658702236407862723316269191967

Mark and count: 723

4824241503857068603304505234755656388752037437232039376974634539514388949756344713567232231417239826399142981568167234873732807236571428946305899091276287928808555411975005667564468121189386007237231407238783931357789876347237496541797237233978094376376601215366503263598557237094917233589397231355588101034525596167973279084156121163044067257234638885816116216587022364078627233162691919 67

Are you sure? See page 195!

Now draw the visualized picture again with as many details as possible:

TRY TO REMEMBER!

What should you find?

- River: _____
- Country: _____
- Decrypted text: _____

What words should you memorize?

- Object: _____
- Activity: _____

day 8

WARM UP!

REMEMBER THE OBJECT: scissors

$9 \cdot 4 =$ ___	$8 + 7 + 12 =$ ___
$7 + 4 =$ ___	$22 - 13 - 3 =$ ___
$3 \cdot 6 =$ ___	$4 + 9 + 10 =$ ___
$4 \cdot 5 =$ ___	$7 + 18 - 17 =$ ___
$15 - 8 =$ ___	$12 + 5 + 6 =$ ___
$5 + 11 =$ ___	$6 + 8 + 16 =$ ___
$5 \cdot 6 =$ ___	$21 - 13 - 6 =$ ___
$10 \cdot 4 =$ ___	$12 + 7 - 7 =$ ___
$13 + 7 =$ ___	$13 + 22 - 5 =$ ___
$6 + 13 =$ ___	$20 - 4 - 15 =$ ___
$2 + 17 =$ ___	$15 + 4 + 9 =$ ___
$5 \cdot 3 =$ ___	$5 + 4 + 15 =$ ___
$7 + 3 =$ ___	$14 + 5 + 8 =$ ___
$5 \cdot 7 =$ ___	$16 + 21 - 9 =$ ___
$11 - 11 =$ ___	$9 + 12 + 6 =$ ___
$20 - 5 =$ ___	$30 - 15 - 4 =$ ___
$18 - 16 =$ ___	$29 - 18 - 9 =$ ___
$8 \cdot 9 =$ ___	$30 - 10 - 17 =$ ___
$5 - 2 =$ ___	$20 + 27 - 19 =$ ___
$4 + 10 =$ ___	$17 + 8 - 14 =$ ___

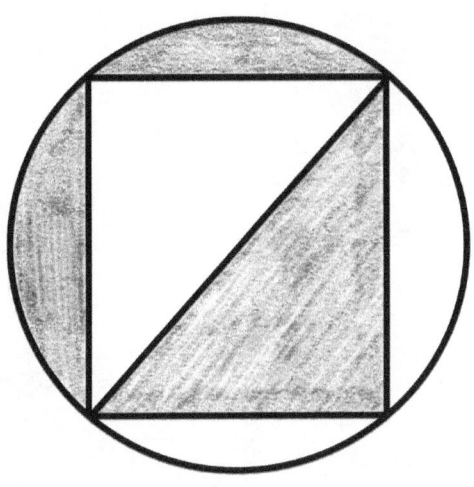

Sketch the picture as precisely as possible and memorize the details so that you can draw it again later:

36	27
11	6
18	23
20	8
7	23
16	30
30	2
40	12
20	30
19	1
19	28
15	24
10	27
35	28
0	27
15	11
2	2
72	3
3	28
14	11

```
Decipher the following code:

X W G N B O
3 4 2 4 5 1
4 5 6 5 4 2

- - - - - -
- - - - - -
6 5 2 1 4 3

Original text: (turn the page)
- - - - - -
1 2 3 4 5 6

ABCDEFGHIJKLMNOPQRSTUVWXYZ_ABCDEFGHIJ
```

Mark and count: INDUS

```
INDUSUSDINDUUIDDDNDSUNDUNUNSNSUUNSN
UIIDDNNDIINDUSSNUISNINDUSDIINDUSIUI
ISUIIIUSNSIDUINDUSUUNDUNNIUNSSDUDUS
DDDNSUIUSDUDSIISIIIDDDISINSSUNSIUID
SINDUSUDUSUSDNSSSISNINNDINDUSNDNINI
UNNSSINDUSNSIUINDUSSUUUSDUNSDSNSUUU
DNNSSUSDUSUININNNINDUSUUUUNNNNDSDDD
DUUINDUSNDNDNNSSSDNNNUNUNISISDIDISI
DDDNINDUSDUDSDUSINSSSUIUUISUINNUUII
UUDUNDDUINDUSUDDNUNDSUNIIINDUSISSNN
DDNINDUSIDDUINDUSSDNSSNNDNSINDUSDUD
IDDNINUINDUSSDINDUSNINDUSIUNUUSUDII
UISINSNIISUUUINDUSNSDDNUSDIDSSUDNDD
```

day 8

Mark and count: MEXICO

```
FTLHJUPZMEXICOYNKQFWTYFVMMXUNDXXZIF          5    9
BMEXICOFIZFPMPEMEXICOOVXESGCZMEXICO         20   21
MEXICONYAWLFLMEXICOUFNCUDMEXICOVIFX         45   39
MVEUZCZNRDYFVCRUNVGNKPGBMEXICOEAULS         12   12
ZNRFJOMEXICOURIQRTPBAMYBXJHMEXICOPE         16    0
SQTLMEXICOTXMGSUVMRKUMEXICOXUWRUGZS         24    2
OBAHLEWBFBCLTVHLZQTQMEXICOXQSPPOLIF         30   33
GLFGDVHIIBUYBMHBLMEXICOJJAMYBCPZGNV         21   41
BMEXICOCHGMEXICOSIATHHCYUCMEXICOUQI         45   44
YXXYNYGMEXICORUMEXICOMUXJLBCMUIMXJG         23   49
ALMEXICOODMOCHFRWMEXICOUJJHJIVWCMNY          2   10
AWMEXICORHLQQBXBPLFRZPVZSEFMQBEVFPJ          5   12
UWCYMEXICOYYPXMMEXICOPMEXICOHJGKKDT          7   39
PEKROBNEJRFWTNQNMYKJATUYWIHPWUNFCGM         90   48
MEXICOWDBYJULZUPCISFNCXZIUHHRNOSCOA         13   30
WCVUDGJFGYMEXICOHSSOFPWBBDEPNTVSCIV         22   28
CPCEBETKPGFQEKBQKFWOMEXICOCMKRRHUEM         13   10
YZLKWYVSAXHZMEXICOTXGYYFKEJJGUBOMYH         11    9
DFQJYWMEXICOPRTABLMEXICOVVNMEXICOLS         15   31
NPETGQDJAEKXSOTXQWHNLUYIANAUMEXICON          0   39
ATTMEXICOYBXAEMUPABYEEDNWMKJNKEHGEN
WDDRHIVYAATLRXHQYUHWZWPXZQLYUMIDIRB
HMBPSDQLLMEXICOXVFHZKFMEXICOVCEQEFQ
WFZHZENJVYMEXICOPYUQJODCBREXXMEXICO
JAVSJCVNBNXGFWOQSAFEMEXICOSPKNTBFOW
WFOENADIMNTSTZKHPQMEXICORMEXICOKLZX
MEXICOBDCNXVYYPOXPQMLRMVMEXICOMOVZA
SRISTITAMEXICOYDXSSYRHZILMEXICOTEEZ
MANZCWTVWEGESNUWKESHZLDQMGERBLIHUEK
```

Are you sure? See page 194.
Copy the decrypted text on page 197.

CALCULATE

REMEMBER THE ACTIVITY: wrestling

$22 - 21 =$ _____

$2 \cdot 4 =$ _____

$7 \cdot 6 =$ _____

$25 + 14 =$ _____

$14 + 24 =$ _____

$26 + 11 =$ _____

$27 + 24 =$ _____

$7 \cdot 8 =$ _____

$33 - 18 =$ _____

$31 - 11 =$ _____

$4 \cdot 10 =$ _____

$18 - 8 =$ _____

$23 + 15 =$ _____

$34 - 12 =$ _____

$28 - 8 =$ _____

$32 - 30 =$ _____

$8 \cdot 2 =$ _____

$23 + 27 =$ _____

$19 - 5 =$ _____

$31 - 20 =$ _____

$6 \cdot 10 - 32 =$ _____

$42 - 27 - 7 =$ _____

$49 + 9 + 39 =$ _____

$34 + 49 - 34 =$ _____

$3 \cdot 5 + 36 =$ _____

$6 \cdot 9 + 45 =$ _____

$58 + 18 + 19 =$ _____

$7 + 38 + 14 =$ _____

$59 + 13 - 29 =$ _____

$8 \cdot 4 - 32 =$ _____

$10 \cdot 6 - 6 =$ _____

$10 \cdot 9 - 34 =$ _____

$32 - 16 - 12 =$ _____

$21 + 45 - 42 =$ _____

$30 + 47 + 9 =$ _____

$8 \cdot 5 - 29 =$ _____

$12 + 40 + 16 =$ _____

$8 \cdot 8 - 53 =$ _____

$30 + 16 - 23 =$ _____

$8 \cdot 2 - 7 =$ _____

Additional tasks - only for math lovers!

24 - 19 = ____	25 + 4 - 20 = ____
8 + 12 = ____	7 • 7 - 28 = ____
9 • 5 = ____	9 • 2 + 21 = ____
3 • 4 = ____	5 + 4 + 3 = ____
2 • 8 = ____	22 - 17 - 5 = ____
3 • 8 = ____	13 + 16 - 27 = ____
5 • 6 = ____	3 • 3 + 24 = ____
3 • 7 = ____	10 • 5 - 9 = ____
5 • 9 = ____	27 + 23 - 6 = ____
5 + 18 = ____	28 + 9 + 12 = ____
9 - 7 = ____	3 • 7 - 11 = ____
27 - 22 = ____	6 + 24 - 18 = ____
25 - 18 = ____	3 • 5 + 24 = ____
9 • 10 = ____	21 + 6 + 21 = ____
29 - 16 = ____	13 + 13 + 4 = ____
14 + 8 = ____	13 + 9 + 6 = ____
6 + 7 = ____	7 + 30 - 27 = ____
21 - 10 = ____	3 • 8 - 15 = ____
8 + 7 = ____	5 • 10 - 19 = ____
5 - 5 = ____	24 + 12 + 3 = ____

Decrypted original text from the previous page:
WORKED

FIND THE NUMBERS!

1	28
8	8
42	97
39	49
38	51
37	99
51	95
56	59
15	43
20	0
40	54
10	56
38	4
22	24
20	86
2	11
16	68
50	11
14	23
11	9

Mark and count: 71

182319208419624516627485594532
201944739938841845799757183740
712737644339368699105692595848
391126546290699071646466328226
102298291980697511913871763212
781331926228174141506785396082
485429726319846785532495288627
218094589020765428849557712076
684629637534785943765166577124
798578109341406882488722714844
314687304552169194641031266570
624272587450829983525769887570
917135144966278838592163417551

Mark and count: 912

820440164317421856621976544510
499587142725791667659364912973
246202716542985262320286329106
660842386600774848882807514923
612460674393126255141743339367
879534585331740819410872872512
709912131930361501146943866416
156375965912408169333704816530
928302418270217468569588656355
401906109912191891594199667386
721912465616775395177915314460
650912751912923569567701912358
548883791898865633914660948126

Are you sure? See page 195!

Now draw the visualized picture again with as many details as possible:

TRY TO REMEMBER!

What should you find?

- River: _____
- Country: _____
- Decrypted text: _____

What words should you memorize?

- Object: _____
- Activity: _____

day 9

WARM UP!

REMEMBER THE OBJECT: pen

10 + 10 = _____	12 + 6 - 11 = _____
8 • 6 = _____	28 - 3 - 17 = _____
10 • 8 = _____	8 + 11 + 8 = _____
14 + 2 = _____	30 - 12 - 16 = _____
4 • 5 = _____	8 + 17 + 5 = _____
20 - 8 = _____	5 + 15 + 9 = _____
10 + 4 = _____	30 - 12 - 3 = _____
13 - 4 = _____	14 + 5 - 13 = _____
2 • 4 = _____	24 - 5 - 17 = _____
15 - 2 = _____	16 + 6 + 5 = _____
4 + 14 = _____	21 + 12 - 4 = _____
12 - 5 = _____	7 + 14 + 7 = _____
5 • 8 = _____	11 - 5 - 4 = _____
2 + 11 = _____	16 - 6 - 7 = _____
10 • 6 = _____	11 + 8 + 4 = _____
7 - 6 = _____	28 - 21 - 4 = _____
5 + 10 = _____	23 - 16 - 4 = _____
14 - 8 = _____	14 - 5 - 4 = _____
15 + 5 = _____	13 + 6 - 16 = _____
17 - 4 = _____	14 + 5 - 17 = _____

Sketch the picture as precisely as possible and memorize the details so that you can draw it again later:

WORDS AND LETTERS

20	7
48	8
80	27
16	2
20	30
12	29
14	15
9	6
8	2
13	27
18	29
7	28
40	2
13	3
60	23
1	3
15	3
6	5
20	3
13	2

```
Decipher the following code:

O  S  Q  H  C  D  R  H
4  3  4  3  3  3  2  1
1  6  2  1  2  2  7  3

—  —  —  —  —  —  —  —
—  —  —  —  —  —  —  —
3  6  1  7  4  2  5  8

Original text: (turn the page)
—  —  —  —  —  —  —  —
1  2  3  4  5  6  7  8

ABCDEFGHIJKLMNOPQRSTUVWXYZ_ABCDEFGHIJ
```

Mark and count: EUPHRATES

```
SRHTUATTHPUEEUPHRATESEPHHEEAEUSASST
UEUPHRATESTEUEEUPHRATESHPHARUUUUEPU
REHEERETHEEUPHRATESHEHTUSSRRRPTUSAR
ESTRTEPAPAESEPRTURPERAPTEUHTHHEAHRR
TSSUEUPHRATESEHHUEEAEUPHRATESTHRUSE
SEEPAUESSUREUPHRATESSEPHTRTREEAAEES
HEPRTEHEPTTRAREAPUHPAETETEUPHRATESP
EPAUAPEHRPEUPHRATESPHAAEHSEUPHRATES
EUPHRATESUTTTTTHHUSASEHAAUEREUAAEAE
ESHPAATTTUARTHPHEUPHRATESTUEERPSEH
TPREERRAPRPSARUEPHTEUTEEHAPUHAASERT
USUPHPEHAERPESAEHEUPHRATESHTSPRSETE
HATEHHEUPHRATESSEAHHUEUPHRATESURESE
```

Mark and count: BRAZIL

```
ZTQILYULOMHPFSQDOULSDJCOATUKWCBIEWA
ONWJUDWNXTEJTGACJIWLJGUJQRNENBFBHVU
GHBRAZILEAZRWBRAZILXPRERFSOXQVJXWUF
PVXADSETLUPKWDLVZNDPAWJVZTDBBDTECPG
MJOBRAZILBMRQDEWRHIGQEOUYGEDGWHMGBN
IDJKQRUZGJVMSBEOVGRQLLQTPREBRGFUFIP
RAVCFSKMCHOJMBQZGIZDCPBRAZILAVXAOMX
VCKDUXBKEBRAZILMKBRAZILQFSYQFYTJLUO
FFLOYLNDSAWLOHLNQIXDUKKUEMDHLBRAZIL
XBRAZILQJVHSWKZVXICRBRAZILMBRAZILJG
WGABACVFIULXCSAHDYTRAGYHZWSGHJLNMGN
DCFZXHPSBRAZILICMZEQWMULEQPTBRAZILT
JZBQWMOPTAKIBRAZILZXGXYKEBRAZILOJQV
BRAZILOBRAZILOAEKXWSSHUCOBYLNZWFCNG
OUKSZBRAZILISYUILPUBTLJHNUHJJQCHOCR
DVCAICCNIBRAZILOKBEAHVYBDPMQGIDRLYL
BKVBRAZILBRAZILTCAZHJTNNCHPJLFUSPZL
RCPBRAZILBRAZILUMNWNAWAYFNVMQWZRTBT
BCFEDBRAZILNRCIFUGAVEJTYHYBRAZILPUZ
OFWJBRAZILJRFCVDBRAZILBQQLHSJFCAVYX
GLVNOMYMBRAZILTSBBRAZILQXFOHXOTWPJH
WRHKKMBRAZILVJBIFUXMICJMAPAIZDLLQCD
QNLRBRAZILWTMWFTBZEKIZVZAIEUILLIQLU
BRAZILATQDKHXLJQEWZFBRAZILFBRAZILDD
MMHPYJERVJZDZCGDPJNQNHLBRAZILLYIOEC
IGKOJTORMPBRAZILIJOCNAVSLQRMQJCGMQK
ADLMKMJQPJLNCYJFDPTZGSVPIXIQBFJZPQD
ZOXKMUFVBRAZILIEXCVJEBRAZILDSVBUAKX
DEZSBRAZILLCTBRAZILAVFJHKTEPPCRKGOX
```

6	9
23	23
18	20
14	29
22	34
10	45
15	43
8	35
2	4
11	3
8	39
16	12
12	7
0	41
21	0
32	27
54	42
29	22
20	25
13	28

Are you sure? See page 194.
Copy the decrypted text on page 197.

CALCULATE

REMEMBER THE ACTIVITY: jogging

23 + 23 = _____	22 - 9 - 7 = _____
10 • 2 = _____	8 • 5 - 27 = _____
40 - 29 = _____	23 + 12 + 36 = _____
2 • 8 = _____	28 + 31 + 17 = _____
6 + 11 = _____	9 • 4 + 41 = _____
27 + 23 = _____	9 • 6 - 16 = _____
9 + 25 = _____	46 + 40 + 6 = _____
3 • 10 = _____	7 + 15 + 37 = _____
17 + 11 = _____	59 + 26 - 23 = _____
9 + 19 = _____	27 - 6 - 12 = _____
21 - 14 = _____	9 + 34 + 7 = _____
18 + 22 = _____	46 + 26 - 21 = _____
32 - 12 = _____	14 + 16 + 46 = _____
9 • 4 = _____	9 • 9 + 11 = _____
7 + 15 = _____	9 • 2 + 50 = _____
11 + 21 = _____	17 + 16 + 26 = _____
5 • 5 = _____	30 + 34 - 43 = _____
40 - 13 = _____	9 • 2 + 31 = _____
3 • 3 = _____	50 + 26 - 29 = _____
9 • 5 = _____	8 • 7 - 16 = _____

day 9

Additional tasks - only for math lovers!

18 - 12 = ____ 15 + 9 - 15 = ____
17 + 6 = ____ 10 • 5 - 27 = ____
2 • 9 = ____ 5 • 9 - 25 = ____
18 - 4 = ____ 6 • 8 - 19 = ____
6 + 16 = ____ 5 • 10 - 16 = ____
30 - 20 = ____ 8 • 6 - 3 = ____
8 + 7 = ____ 2 • 7 + 29 = ____
2 • 4 = ____ 4 • 3 + 23 = ____
14 - 12 = ____ 4 + 24 - 24 = ____
23 - 12 = ____ 22 - 5 - 14 = ____
22 - 14 = ____ 12 + 10 + 17 = ____
9 + 7 = ____ 2 • 3 + 6 = ____
4 • 3 = ____ 10 + 13 - 16 = ____
3 - 3 = ____ 3 • 5 + 26 = ____
12 + 9 = ____ 9 - 5 - 4 = ____
4 • 8 = ____ 7 • 2 + 13 = ____
6 • 9 = ____ 3 • 8 + 18 = ____
6 + 23 = ____ 13 + 27 - 18 = ____
6 + 14 = ____ 7 • 5 - 10 = ____
24 - 11 = ____ 12 + 20 - 4 = ____

Decrypted original text from the previous page:
WITH ALL

FIND THE NUMBERS!

46	6
20	13
11	71
16	76
17	77
50	38
34	92
30	59
28	62
28	9
7	50
40	51
20	76
36	92
22	68
32	59
25	21
27	49
9	47
45	40

Mark and count: 89

```
68223041204789276334977459481 8
90358216527089575048898689234 3
94964878299895838415638394277 6
65149162479817417280196197746 9
89427528705745969957342851457 9
39828029509554606712734793259 5
69671969283082131490502652888 7
32663429682511947374628727627 2
22819645248965448885374655683
35433832968674618558302716898 9
89353798701685167682242459898 9
33374855773361292765512252241 4
88314545935886895260573687775 8
```

Mark and count: 336

```
32077084691021687734438512876 0
35876320570279025093355729915 2
96196131795783063145165115718 7
89867195753487863065731614059 2
38767141242979782939077770536 7
52564712593014683823186976662 9
33624256528952445262969816097 3
10665931994457373179533618513 7
84654496552433662889636289542 5
44427367657798458052129493475 5
88366198639774748612833641160 8
76992913945092289111183426533 6
92082546628926778672844832257 0
```

Are you sure? See page 195!

Now draw the visualized picture again with as many details as possible:

TRY TO REMEMBER!

What should you find?

- River: _____
- Country: _____
- Decrypted text: _____

What words should you memorize?

- Object: _____
- Activity: _____

day 10

WARM UP!

REMEMBER THE OBJECT: computer

11 + 9 = ____	21 + 4 - 21 = ____
5 • 8 = ____	27 - 21 - 3 = ____
14 + 5 = ____	23 + 18 - 18 = ____
7 • 8 = ____	20 + 18 - 17 = ____
2 • 8 = ____	5 + 14 + 7 = ____
7 • 10 = ____	27 - 20 - 7 = ____
4 + 7 = ____	8 + 5 + 8 = ____
20 - 7 = ____	4 + 5 + 17 = ____
13 + 7 = ____	13 + 26 - 26 = ____
17 - 14 = ____	28 + 8 - 19 = ____
7 + 2 = ____	23 + 23 - 24 = ____
14 - 7 = ____	18 + 21 - 16 = ____
12 - 7 = ____	5 + 6 + 8 = ____
20 - 16 = ____	20 - 3 - 4 = ____
5 • 10 = ____	4 + 7 + 6 = ____
18 - 8 = ____	23 + 8 - 24 = ____
16 - 15 = ____	6 + 12 + 9 = ____
3 • 2 = ____	8 + 11 - 13 = ____
2 + 3 = ____	4 + 7 + 7 = ____
8 + 5 = ____	24 - 13 - 10 = ____

Sketch the picture as precisely as possible and memorize the details so that you can draw it again later:

20	4
40	3
19	23
56	21
16	26
70	0
11	21
13	26
20	13
3	17
9	22
7	23
5	19
4	13
50	17
10	7
1	27
6	6
5	18
13	1

Decipher the following code:

```
N _ Y E L C _ H P Y M T L
6 1 4 1 4 6 5 2 3 4 1 4 6
2 4 3 7 2 3 3 5 2 3 6 3 1

- - - - - - - - - - - - -
- - - - - - - - - - - - -
7 12 5 11 3 9 2 8 10 4 1 6 13
```

Original text: (turn the page)

```
- - - - - - - - - - - - -
1  2  3  4  5  6  7  8  9  10 11 12 13
```

```
ABCDEFGHIJKLMNOPQRSTUVWXYZ_ABCDEFGHIJ
```

Mark and count: TIGRIS

```
ISISTIGRISSSGSIITSSRRITTIGRISSSSSTS
TRSIISTSIGIRRRGITRRIIGSIIGGSIIRISSI
TISIGGIGIITTIGRISRIITSITSSSTSISGTRI
ITSTIIIITRITGIRIRIIRGGTIGRISISISSGSTT
GRIRRIRRGISTTTTTTIGRISTGISIIGTIGRIS
IIISGIISTITSSTIIITRIIRGIGSIIRITIRIT
TISGGTGTIGRISTRIRTIGRISRIITIGRISRRG
GTRRTITRGITGGISSIIRIIGRIRIIIITIGRIS
ISRIITTRGITISTIGRISSGGSTIISSTGIRRRI
ITITIRGGGSSIRTTIRIITSRGITSIIGRRISIS
TIRGSITIGRISITGISTIGRISIISSSSISISSG
TSGTITGSGSTIGRISTIGRISSRITRTSTRTISS
IITSRSSSSTSSRTISIIIITIGIITIGRISSGTR
```

Mark and count: ARGENTINA

```
CFARGENTINAKQVSPARGENTINABTEHXLUQZZ
OGQZMVILYBARGENTINAQWWXDDZRRYFBXSAE
EARGENTINAXSFARGENTINAARGENTINAIRNH
HDGCXAOCLJIYZPEEAMARGENTINAXLANPIYI
BTTOUJDCARGENTINAEJXQKYINPZLQPRFERK
EARGENTINAMWLTMCFKRDTEKDXSFGSNXDHLL
JELVAMJFQBPKEARGENTINAXWHXARGENTINA
VSALQHATJASBCXEFEARGENTINABJAZEQVMQ
VCXZXLRSWAIGZYARGENTINASCXRRIZIAJIL
JTFHZPJYXRAGRDDNPTZOWKSLUMSCPFIJDXH
TWVRTQFARGENTINAVGFIHAAILRJKTQUZCXR
VZDAHCZKVAHNSARGENTINAARGENTINATRLI
ILMARGENTINAGGIFVMARGENTINASKHZAKPW
TJTNZBLDBUARGENTINALRAJARGENTINATPW
CARGENTINARXSBWARGENTINABEAYXMWAMEN
TRJQMLLQXEBGCARGENTINAXCUYTIEBVPUIJ
MFTARGENTINASGTOMLKMRMHBLARGENTINAS
QSKCZWKLFKARGENTINAVIWKGWSPOCQBPHZM
YSIZAPPJZZXIDSJARGENTINAOGARGENTINA
ZFFARGENTINAMADFMSPARGENTINAFKLACVM
IRLLLWGZVARGENTINAAKFDMFFIKVVDHOPAL
OJKUEPALOGKARGENTINADWMQUARGENTINAZ
AARGENTINALBFXEARGENTINAARGENTINAZF
EYZWVARGENTINAOLQQIESERRSVRMRUZNQKH
FAPAEOTWNXNRJBTYARGENTINAOVIPVDLOVC
QUUNWTARGENTINAXVDHQVVAARGENTINAMQL
BQGZARGENTINATCRQCANJIODIGDRQHOCYRY
WLARGENTINAXOSDVARGENTINAHGKGZLQRLV
ARGENTINAYXICNLEBMHNWFARGENTINACCWB
```

9	10
20	11
18	49
42	46
2	29
28	17
40	39
7	1
9	19
21	24
45	27
0	45
63	48
24	37
14	44
90	24
19	34
36	3
10	21
11	8

Are you sure? See page 194.
Copy the decrypted text on page 197.

CALCULATE

REMEMBER THE ACTIVITY: surfing

17 + 17 = _____	2 • 4 + 49 = _____
23 + 13 = _____	7 • 9 + 27 = _____
9 + 27 = _____	34 + 18 - 24 = _____
6 - 6 = _____	30 + 55 - 44 = _____
8 • 7 = _____	30 + 58 - 4 = _____
19 - 15 = _____	9 • 7 - 16 = _____
18 + 23 = _____	5 • 10 - 25 = _____
28 + 14 = _____	19 + 26 + 10 = _____
24 + 11 = _____	6 • 8 - 17 = _____
8 • 9 = _____	6 • 9 + 14 = _____
40 - 33 = _____	46 - 27 - 13 = _____
28 - 25 = _____	53 + 38 - 39 = _____
22 - 10 = _____	12 + 57 + 24 = _____
39 - 22 = _____	5 • 9 + 29 = _____
4 • 2 = _____	5 • 7 + 44 = _____
14 + 13 = _____	36 + 29 - 56 = _____
5 • 2 = _____	20 + 10 + 12 = _____
22 - 21 = _____	40 - 19 - 15 = _____
21 + 7 = _____	52 + 57 - 38 = _____
16 - 10 = _____	46 + 6 - 27 = _____

> Additional tasks - only for math lovers!

23 - 14 = ____	30 - 9 - 11 = ____
5 • 4 = ____	22 - 5 - 6 = ____
9 • 2 = ____	25 + 19 + 5 = ____
7 • 6 = ____	6 • 4 + 22 = ____
24 - 22 = ____	2 • 3 + 23 = ____
7 • 4 = ____	3 • 10 - 13 = ____
8 • 5 = ____	23 + 7 + 9 = ____
13 - 6 = ____	16 - 7 - 8 = ____
13 - 4 = ____	3 • 10 - 11 = ____
26 - 5 = ____	4 • 10 - 16 = ____
9 • 5 = ____	8 • 7 - 29 = ____
30 - 30 = ____	26 + 10 + 9 = ____
9 • 7 = ____	21 + 3 + 24 = ____
3 • 8 = ____	7 + 9 + 21 = ____
2 • 7 = ____	2 • 10 + 24 = ____
9 • 10 = ____	3 • 5 + 9 = ____
13 + 6 = ____	4 • 7 + 6 = ____
9 • 4 = ____	3 • 6 - 15 = ____
14 - 4 = ____	28 + 6 - 13 = ____
21 - 10 = ____	17 + 12 - 21 = ____

Decrypted original text from the previous page:
THREE VOLUMES

FIND THE NUMBERS!

34	57
36	90
36	28
0	41
56	84
4	47
41	25
42	55
35	31
72	68
7	6
3	52
12	93
17	74
8	79
27	9
10	42
1	6
28	71
6	25

Mark and count: 82

57599353181441498322826723 6145
82176425809222755764328982 1440
32666931344844863490297196 5711
58578039823440139859181882 3324
61212369956114332142571966 9446
44867893864141495291951782 9684
65823579582987823955724585 7034
67875021229016561991385936 8212
77872217479764543468433980 2094
79346081825727402365827749 6010
56378224279582789735954757 6888
23948582552418643451828479 2266
55956334284840342838706787 6532

Mark and count: 556

38330410242364225551084533 0973
10030846853930785684576523 5140
15675143931077266648291455 6871
60447054027454755628288915 6815
87767299147567229861976333 0957
38933183346161876955636253 2964
22269298662736430091749055 6151
58750283553034437171594894 3970
11450791489462498150644049 9802
62880680755612714749399866 4394
91311315454788827552245024 9956
96683486393334692264844238 4556
93237817955644111536960529 0779

Are you sure? See page 195!

Now draw the visualized picture again with as many details as possible:

TRY TO REMEMBER!

What should you find?

- River: _____
- Country: _____
- Decrypted text: _____

What words should you memorize?

- Object: _____
- Activity: _____

day 11

WARM UP!

REMEMBER THE OBJECT: book

2 + 2 = _____	25 - 14 - 5 = _____
5 + 4 = _____	15 - 3 - 3 = _____
10 - 5 = _____	8 + 6 + 14 = _____
4 · 2 = _____	4 + 8 - 9 = _____
17 - 12 = _____	15 + 5 + 8 = _____
8 - 4 = _____	8 + 18 - 4 = _____
6 · 5 = _____	8 + 5 + 7 = _____
4 + 7 = _____	29 - 15 - 7 = _____
17 + 3 = _____	11 + 7 + 9 = _____
6 - 2 = _____	19 + 4 + 4 = _____
19 - 15 = _____	18 + 8 + 4 = _____
8 - 8 = _____	9 + 12 + 9 = _____
6 - 5 = _____	18 + 8 - 24 = _____
5 + 8 = _____	5 + 10 + 13 = _____
19 - 4 = _____	15 + 11 + 4 = _____
3 · 6 = _____	30 - 3 - 23 = _____
2 + 6 = _____	26 + 15 - 11 = _____
16 - 12 = _____	10 + 21 - 17 = _____
14 + 5 = _____	9 + 14 + 7 = _____
3 · 10 = _____	20 + 20 - 24 = _____

Sketch the picture as precisely as possible and memorize the details so that you can draw it again later:

4	6
9	9
5	28
8	3
5	28
4	22
30	20
11	7
20	27
4	27
4	30
0	30
1	2
13	28
15	30
18	4
8	30
4	14
19	30
30	16

Decipher the following code:

```
U  Z  L  M  G  B  K  _  K  N
1  5  6  3  1  4  5  3  3  3
5  4  1  4  7  3  3  5  5  6

_  _  _  _  _  _  _  _  _  _

_  _  _  _  _  _  _  _  _  _
5  2  6  1  8  3  4  7  10 9
```

Original text: (turn the page)

```
_  _  _  _  _  _  _  _  _  _
1  2  3  4  5  6  7  8  9  10
```

ABCDEFGHIJKLMNOPQRSTUVWXYZ_ABCDEFGHIJ

Mark and count: CONGO

```
OOGCOGNCOCGCOGGGCONGOCCCNCNOCCGCCNN
GGOGCCONGOCNONONNCONGOOCONCOOCONGOO
CCOOOCNOOOCCNOOGNNGOCONGONONCOOONOC
ONOCONGOGNOOCONGOOOONCONGOOOGOOCOOC
COCNOOONCNOOCOOOOCNNCCONGONOCONGOON
OOONOCONGOCONGOCOOCCOGGNCONGOGOGNNG
OOOCNOCONGOOOGGCOGOCOOONGCNONCGOCOO
NGONCOGCNOOGOGOCONGOCGOOGNCONGOOOCC
OOOCOOOONOGCCNOONGNNOGOGCNGNCONGONO
OCCNOCNONOCCGNNGCOONOCOGCONGOGNGOON
OCONGONCONGOCOOOOOCONGONGNCONOOONOO
ONNOCONGONNCNCCOCONGOOOCCCONGOCGONC
NOCONGOOCNCCOCONGONCOCGNOOCONONNGGO
```

118

Mark and count: CHILE

IYNXCHILEVIITORSQNBLGRZFBDPMCHILEMK
FJMGADKMESRSYNSTAVPTCHILEVCHILEVOZH
XVCCOMUYFAPNWZYTCEMPQMSCHILEPGJVJQE
RTTCHILEDDJCDTTRKZXBSAXLWZKXVKPWTZG
QYKPIOWSKGOQCHILEGGCHILEPVBCHILERIF
XWVZJMQZWSXCHILENOXZCHILEIBEFERNAOK
ADCCSNFVCHILESFMIWPMVRSXZCCZIMBTKHS
QLTMVWIJRCHILEYUZZMHGHGVEEDKHTBJOPL
YWVJDHDEIWIFACCHILEEGCHILEROPNAYYQL
EKSKJAZLSRNFCOYSHWPBBBCHILEQICYVTAG
SUAYGLRCHILESLZLSSAPQEXFDLLPAYAWASX
WUPIVBOQLFPXFSQCHILEEUXWRMFWKAEVCIS
UVPXLACHILEKWOUNFJZMKLQUKGXHWOXNLBY
YGMRCECHILESTVKZIZFWLFJKTSUJCCHILEI
WZAQRBJRACHILEANPRTDPSJMOOKQORSKBSJ
TCHILECHILEZKUQCHILECHILEDADIVPJRXB
XTXMSKWOGNKURNWDTMQUQRYMZKIWMCHILEG
QCHILEJLLUQQVINYUTSONQIFOJMIKMXPRSN
ENCHILEVACQVQSUVRTTUECHILEVUFUPXXBH
HSYHIRCHILEECOTWNXEZVCECMWZRNUAKTPT
MKNCHILETVCPZASCHILEDEOFWLICHILEACM
EDHYYOABWPWSRCJGKPNJOZZNUDDXOQKDTJA
MVEWOXOXNCOHUWMOHMILPXBODTAYHFUSERJ
LFCEOCKVCHILEVAPCCHILENZFDBGTQSKFCB
VKGVBOFXIPOULPCHILESUYHQNEHNNLIKVAV
JSGQCWSDASDJIGJEHSCHILENCHILEXRXEFP
INBGLLQGISDJHNWGNKKMFNXTZDMSYMYRJBC
DMHXZWVCHILEFFCHILEFCOEANFRXORDPOYD
QWICHILECSYACHILENYQCMMSUKXRETRANLR

16	17
0	38
42	34
42	45
30	27
30	32
23	10
0	34
24	44
8	44
13	16
23	9
14	8
20	35
54	39
25	7
5	9
9	17
26	35
16	6

Are you sure? See page 194.
Copy the decrypted text on page 197.

CALCULATE

REMEMBER THE ACTIVITY: hang gliding

25 + 30 = _____   53 - 11 - 34 = _____

17 + 16 = _____   5 • 7 - 6 = _____

4 • 10 = _____   41 + 42 - 48 = _____

5 • 8 = _____   9 • 8 - 48 = _____

14 - 12 = _____   4 • 8 + 21 = _____

40 - 28 = _____   40 - 12 - 24 = _____

2 • 10 = _____   12 + 21 + 29 = _____

6 • 6 = _____   4 • 3 + 60 = _____

22 - 21 = _____   20 + 11 + 7 = _____

3 • 4 = _____   27 + 18 + 53 = _____

27 - 21 = _____   53 + 22 - 14 = _____

8 • 5 = _____   8 • 4 - 31 = _____

18 - 5 = _____   17 + 47 - 54 = _____

26 + 7 = _____   26 + 23 + 22 = _____

20 - 18 = _____   27 + 32 - 4 = _____

7 + 27 = _____   52 + 20 + 22 = _____

16 + 30 = _____   9 • 5 + 8 = _____

6 • 2 = _____   5 • 2 + 31 = _____

4 • 9 = _____   9 • 5 + 15 = _____

32 - 13 = _____   53 - 26 - 7 = _____

Additional tasks - only for math lovers!

8 • 2 = ____   23 + 20 - 26 = ____

19 - 19 = ____   28 + 15 - 5 = ____

7 • 6 = ____   24 + 15 - 5 = ____

6 • 7 = ____   12 + 15 + 18 = ____

5 • 6 = ____   4 + 15 + 8 = ____

6 • 5 = ____   2 • 7 + 18 = ____

16 + 7 = ____   26 - 6 - 10 = ____

9 - 9 = ____   2 • 3 + 28 = ____

4 • 6 = ____   9 + 20 + 15 = ____

20 - 12 = ____   8 • 3 + 20 = ____

22 - 9 = ____   5 • 5 - 9 = ____

18 + 5 = ____   23 - 7 - 7 = ____

8 + 6 = ____   21 - 10 - 3 = ____

12 + 8 = ____   23 + 22 - 10 = ____

6 • 9 = ____   18 + 17 + 4 = ____

11 + 14 = ____   28 - 3 - 18 = ____

13 - 8 = ____   4 + 26 - 21 = ____

23 - 14 = ____   26 - 3 - 6 = ____

7 + 19 = ____   29 + 11 - 5 = ____

11 + 5 = ____   28 - 11 - 11 = ____

Decrypted original text from the previous page:
THIS SHOWS

FIND THE NUMBERS!

55	8
33	29
40	35
40	24
2	53
12	4
20	62
36	72
1	38
12	98
6	61
40	1
13	10
33	71
2	55
34	94
46	53
12	41
36	60
19	20

Mark and count: 91

39448283443376697071148399795
91674161953084117141187272959 6
27567228502422586416387931339 1
35391945737663516628166347873 9
31552078762895679359275423825 2
32799147402346427891857735956 9
46585355318577551981914858299 2
24689384607439353291127833249 1
64531351895582266424916958931 3
47646426541056585630258611471 9
33529888347141912752024539837
62322521581664347580355589232 7
38309636584764926246168389294 0

Mark and count: 269

46194427254562026987818229255 0
33843924937845097363661248561 1
26984123311690459372916688564 8
26945942995726931830926994557 1
38962618634566796338524690351 9
26968871273689048373226975149 1
92448734426961436744127649456 3
72197855677118638226983288480 1
30336297261684915424277757549 0
10937427140855261784382837310 4
24040684941237065941745356776 8
43096492651030592626756314326 9
97226943930220454266323265575 3

Are you sure? See page 195!

Now draw the visualized picture again with as many details as possible:

TRY TO REMEMBER!

What should you find?

- River: _____
- Country: _____
- Decrypted text: _____

What words should you memorize?

- Object: _____
- Activity: _____

day 12

WARM UP!

REMEMBER THE OBJECT: microphone

4 • 3 = _____	19 + 8 - 26 = _____
17 + 2 = _____	30 - 16 - 5 = _____
18 - 6 = _____	12 + 9 + 9 = _____
6 • 2 = _____	6 + 7 + 16 = _____
2 + 8 = _____	20 + 22 - 17 = _____
7 + 8 = _____	24 + 8 - 5 = _____
5 - 2 = _____	14 + 7 - 6 = _____
5 • 7 = _____	24 + 8 - 24 = _____
10 • 4 = _____	25 + 27 - 27 = _____
9 • 4 = _____	11 + 12 + 6 = _____
2 + 10 = _____	29 - 21 - 7 = _____
9 • 6 = _____	20 + 23 - 17 = _____
12 + 6 = _____	9 + 9 + 11 = _____
6 + 3 = _____	5 + 4 + 8 = _____
20 - 13 = _____	24 + 14 - 14 = _____
4 + 12 = _____	9 + 5 + 12 = _____
10 • 8 = _____	21 + 8 - 24 = _____
9 • 8 = _____	26 + 18 - 24 = _____
18 - 10 = _____	5 + 5 + 5 = _____
9 + 4 = _____	29 - 14 - 13 = _____

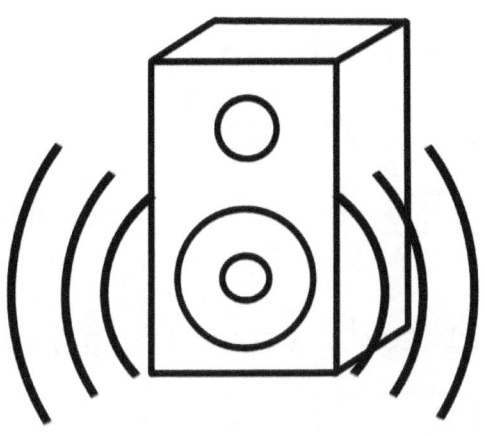

Sketch the picture as precisely as possible and memorize the details so that you can draw it again later:

12	1
19	9
12	30
12	29
10	25
15	27
3	15
35	8
40	25
36	29
12	1
54	26
18	29
9	17
7	24
16	26
80	5
72	20
8	15
13	2

```
Decipher the following code:

L V M U I K X L _ Q A Z
5 4 3 4 4 3 1 1 4 6 1 1
4 2 4 2 2 4 2 7 4 2 3 1

- - - - - - - - - - -

- - - - - - - - - - -
8 3 1 9 7 11 5 4 2 6 12 10

Original text: (turn the page)

- - - - - - - - - - - -
1 2 3 4 5 6 7 8 9 10 11 12

ABCDEFGHIJKLMNOPQRSTUVWXYZ_ABCDEFGHIJ
```

Mark and count: GANGES

```
ASNSGGAGANGESGNGGGSNEEAGAGSAGESSEEN
GASGANGESGSGGGGGSSSGGEGEGSGGGSEEGEG
SEEAGGSSGEGAGAAENEAGANGESEEEAGSSSGG
GEGGAAANGGEANGNNNGEGSGANGESGAGASSGG
EGGNSGANGESSGNGGNSSGGAEAGGGANGESGSS
AGAGGGGANGESSGGANGESGANGESSGENAGSGE
GSSGNSENSGANGESGGGGEGAASSNGNEGGNEEGA
EGNGAANGEGGGNNGEANGSGSGSEAGANGESSGA
GANGESASNGGNGAENASSSANEGGSNSAAAAGSG
GNGANGESGGANGESAAGGANGESEAEANNGNGGE
EGEGGSGGGANGESGNGGGAGGAEEASGGNGEGAE
SEGANGESGGNEGANGESGNANGANGESGSEGNGA
NAANGGGANGESGGANASGAGGESNAEGGANGESS
```

128

Mark and count: JAPAN

```
VYXLFBTEAJAPANHPJAPANLEPOXNJAPANBYV
GPDIEBRMDBIYCDIPILAYKGWENLGHFEDVJVY
SXGRIPAYSJOTRFHMJLWXJLDNZDFIDWJZVDX
ROMTAQEWLWFBRDWMVAEXGEJMNUZRKJAPANK
CLMLKRZIJAPANHJAPANFVNJJAPANQJAPANL
JAPANKBTHNSUKHQLVQBRMNVUQJMCTXJAPAN
ABCAZDJAPANMCBILGFDBLKIOYQPUURJAPAN
VQXHYUIDKWVBOHDDKJAPANEWKJAPANHVXPX
WVOCOTPVJTKXEWMSYGWKRZHBXTYDKODHQJS
EJAPANQPBGAGSTPJNFHJSCGMRHCBBDFHCBK
RNNVXYWBRKWUOZBEWWEUVRIHRUZLICARXIG
WVYBJUYDRODQVBNJRNKPEJIFRJDXEKDVFZN
STJTJAPANMZYHBIGDEJAPANEKNJAPANSIWI
POANTQSGWFTWKBWJZTPZCILUYSDLVBGZLWF
KRWOVUKBZVJAPANUKNAOQCTJAPANRJAPANB
LGNLLVKFEIHUWMFBAGUUHTSBRSBLMCTUBWG
KKJDCFOXMUPXAJAPANLTTUJSJXKXQBNVEQV
VDDFYJTXMQXZPCFXCAFKXTKOMJQLLSDOUZF
RLNLOCMFLFTTBSWLRDJAPANMANGEHWCASHO
BXVPYSPLEROPQHWOWERUNDJDBYDXZBKJVKK
IXLRDQHZHYHTFFOPSETHKWDUOTSJAPANDFU
QXGOPAQRZJAPANKLHNBXXGYLIEEECYXOGVF
OZAGEZJGUTBFDYDJWLNKCRGGLJPQVGGHWVG
RPBOKSUGLBUYMYZOUQMAORHMOMXLEHVXUWM
JAPANDYRBUDGVZONUXNUYSJAPANJAPANFTV
FLBCEGKMJBUHRGFTMETIMRNSNJEOGXHYHKT
AIUXPNRPDTBAJAPANVVQTZFXJAPANCHISVM
SJAPANANWDTYJLJUKHYAFHIPGOZOGBGWSGA
JMYGPLOYDJVREMLSCIZJAPANMIRBYXYYLQH
```

1	22
18	19
8	45
5	43
30	25
50	5
10	32
1	41
27	18
17	14
12	10
24	15
36	1
30	45
42	31
6	50
14	34
25	44
20	3
16	10

Are you sure? See page 194.
Copy the decrypted text on page 197.

CALCULATE

REMEMBER THE ACTIVITY: bodybuilding

5 • 4 = ____	11 + 33 + 54 = ____
19 - 15 = ____	46 + 14 + 17 = ____
37 - 22 = ____	7 • 9 + 21 = ____
31 - 21 = ____	38 - 23 - 14 = ____
37 - 26 = ____	9 • 3 + 26 = ____
7 • 9 = ____	19 + 41 - 32 = ____
23 - 23 = ____	4 • 3 - 12 = ____
10 • 9 = ____	6 • 9 + 33 = ____
17 + 8 = ____	2 • 10 + 44 = ____
21 + 15 = ____	35 + 46 - 43 = ____
13 + 11 = ____	7 • 6 + 37 = ____
2 • 8 = ____	47 + 6 - 19 = ____
14 + 25 = ____	5 • 2 + 46 = ____
10 • 2 = ____	35 + 55 - 45 = ____
15 - 8 = ____	7 • 5 + 37 = ____
31 - 25 = ____	48 + 21 + 13 = ____
7 • 6 = ____	60 - 12 - 37 = ____
12 + 30 = ____	53 - 17 - 7 = ____
8 • 6 = ____	10 • 8 - 56 = ____
3 • 6 = ____	9 • 8 - 10 = ____

Additional tasks - only for math lovers!

$15 - 14 =$ _____

$6 \cdot 3 =$ _____

$15 - 7 =$ _____

$20 - 15 =$ _____

$5 \cdot 6 =$ _____

$5 \cdot 10 =$ _____

$24 - 14 =$ _____

$30 - 29 =$ _____

$13 + 14 =$ _____

$12 + 5 =$ _____

$25 - 13 =$ _____

$8 + 16 =$ _____

$6 \cdot 6 =$ _____

$10 + 20 =$ _____

$6 \cdot 7 =$ _____

$22 - 16 =$ _____

$9 + 5 =$ _____

$9 + 16 =$ _____

$2 \cdot 10 =$ _____

$8 + 8 =$ _____

$6 \cdot 2 + 10 =$ _____

$3 + 10 + 6 =$ _____

$15 + 23 + 7 =$ _____

$19 + 8 + 16 =$ _____

$8 \cdot 2 + 9 =$ _____

$18 + 10 - 23 =$ _____

$3 \cdot 6 + 14 =$ _____

$28 + 28 - 15 =$ _____

$2 \cdot 2 + 14 =$ _____

$7 \cdot 3 - 7 =$ _____

$7 + 22 - 19 =$ _____

$4 \cdot 2 + 7 =$ _____

$20 - 4 - 15 =$ _____

$4 + 12 + 29 =$ _____

$4 \cdot 3 + 19 =$ _____

$6 \cdot 9 - 4 =$ _____

$13 + 8 + 13 =$ _____

$5 \cdot 3 + 29 =$ _____

$20 - 7 - 10 =$ _____

$5 \cdot 5 - 15 =$ _____

Decrypted original text from the previous page:
THAT YOU ARE

FIND THE NUMBERS!

20	98
4	77
15	84
10	1
11	53
63	28
0	0
90	87
25	64
36	38
24	79
16	34
39	56
20	45
7	72
6	82
42	11
42	29
48	24
18	62

Mark and count: 32

2985219824847279726314426692654361798761489532784781283699836469195075396232767086328164177799101990557010503929972813511322869739727518163252203617323822234014478015393017706358714671595741384835923811353559223240668755814859372833712880646185498251429625653375214332582366169840915187857136733325428655769816396661443962624793743927231326455198017289384664632409263599976197732685542823345

Mark and count: 610

9929057021875318589393597607614217769726079623454204506115734957235717248669665775634549951269551362767232205283485249506182484182175725678346102428457467315292762222357674075556101551391188218816104425496105548808575023096108211238635935391576672673849977147347957483526101901366101987841702915632746837852658154898321092996101813788572848943976544184742865149238083005164297202202663026 10

    Are you sure? See page 195!

Now draw the visualized picture again with as many details as possible:

day 13

WARM UP!

REMEMBER THE OBJECT: shelf

13 + 2 = _____	4 + 12 + 6 = _____
17 - 16 = _____	13 + 14 - 8 = _____
15 + 4 = _____	5 + 6 + 4 = _____
3 • 3 = _____	11 + 7 + 4 = _____
7 • 7 = _____	25 - 6 - 11 = _____
14 - 13 = _____	5 + 7 + 15 = _____
2 • 4 = _____	19 + 9 - 10 = _____
14 - 14 = _____	10 + 8 + 4 = _____
2 • 6 = _____	7 + 10 + 13 = _____
5 + 6 = _____	13 - 4 - 7 = _____
20 - 6 = _____	30 - 6 - 24 = _____
10 + 3 = _____	28 - 12 - 4 = _____
20 - 17 = _____	12 - 3 - 6 = _____
7 • 2 = _____	12 + 28 - 13 = _____
7 + 13 = _____	20 - 6 - 14 = _____
3 • 5 = _____	17 + 25 - 26 = _____
9 - 5 = _____	6 + 8 + 6 = _____
5 • 2 = _____	21 + 19 - 28 = _____
14 - 9 = _____	23 - 5 - 12 = _____
10 • 2 = _____	24 - 3 - 17 = _____

Sketch the picture as precisely as possible and memorize the details so that you can draw it again later:

15	22
1	19
19	15
9	22
49	8
1	27
8	18
0	22
12	30
11	2
14	0
13	12
3	3
14	27
20	0
15	16
4	20
10	12
5	6
20	4

```
Decipher the following code:

G Z M B M F W Z X V
3 3 4 6 3 3 2 3 6 2
4 3 3 1 2 4 7 3 1 7

_ _ _ _ _ _ _ _ _ _
_ _ _ _ _ _ _ _ _ _
8 9 3 7 5 6 2 4 1 10

Original text: (turn the page)
_ _ _ _ _ _ _ _ _ _
1 2 3 4 5 6 7 8 9 10

ABCDEFGHIJKLMNOPQRSTUVWXYZ_ABCDEFGHIJ
```

Mark and count: BRAHMAPUTRA

ARBRRABRAHMAPUTRAABRAHMAPUTRARAMPMM
RPMBRAHMAPUTRAAUTBBRAHMAPUTRARAHMAB
TRPMAAPBUBBRAHMAPUTRAUBRAHMAPUTRARM
URMTBAHUBRATAATABBBAUARHAHATAAHAPAM
ATMAPBBBRAHMAPUTRATMRAARRHAARMTMAAA
ABHPUBAARHBRAHMAPUTRAPATPRMPABAATRH
ABRAHMAPUTRAABRPMPABPAHRAAPBTUAARBA
TATARRBBRAHMAPUTRAAATTRMPAHUPMPHPR
ATBTPBMRTARHPRRURBRAHMAPUTRABRATHPR
ABRAHMAPUTRAABRAHMAPUTRAABBAARUAAMM
AUBARPPARBATUTTRAPRMBBAAUPHARATABRB
BRAHMAPUTRAAMABTRTHABRUURBAHPTMUPPR
AMAPBRAHMAPUTRARBMPRAMHBPUAAUHTURRP

Mark and count: CHINA

```
WOHXXFTJYHCFVXZYMLCHINAKQBWQPLTVJRZ
CQECHINAWCHINANCQCHINAOCHINACISMESZ
SOTMUSYYOGCOEOHYWCHINAHJDJZNEGZDNAV
OUMQNUPGCHINABMBGHZPNAEDAZKLPGVYDRH
AFWJLOFZZTFQCHINAVOHCHINAGVRUNSEGNY
XLCHINAPXCHINAXECHINADDHUZYCHINAMNU
SSLYZDRCTVNJWYODVLGCHINATXRDUJWKFRJ
BBJFSFJMMJZONFZJAZOZCDXNARGPFKPAFAL
XDXAGEVCJFACHINAFJWXNYCHINAIXAYFVYB
PPTINEXGTIHWAEKZLVYRCHINAOLPBCHINAV
ACHINAWCHYBGBKSRASOMGPNCBWFSFCNQHRK
CHINAGYCHINATAPCSRFFVTVCDOONOHFDRKH
RUYCHINAZGHTKVFLPILDLWEMQCHINAJCMTJ
AFGNYCIHIOVKCZNAOXAIHJCHINANXMTNYPH
WQSBCHINAYXELKMPTCHINANVRVZOGJTHYFH
BCPIBBCHINAIYETVSSCHNFBCHINAWRJHXHL
CLXPOJPYRWZTRPPHEPXFBZXKDZOCHINANOD
DICBOPGXLKXIZZTZZHTWCCHINAPGSIUKSOT
UREPFZZQGZTVMFACHINANJJZNPYGRPTSXTF
MCHINAJCHINACICHINASSIEZICXYZAMORMT
VUCSRRFXAOKZGKCBLYCHINAIIBNWIRHMVDS
HQXJKVTKCHWWSXVTWCHINAEWBGXKIJXSJSW
ZFWYMGRSIAMXPZOFTQKCHINAANUTCHINAHP
KKPXEOGKSJULWLXMCHINARPSXZFUIXRSSHN
BSMGPPTYALXIAABFLGOBVOKKBLYBAWGSGDU
GTKCCHLHXBBCVLEQLPLRJTUEBDJFPDHBFFQ
VSEUZBCDTNPDZZOHPFNJXXWYFIRKSMEKGDA
GVZRDTCHINATISWDFZMLZWERTUOZQWPLUAU
CHINAOQTCXFEVJTURJWMNHCHINABDNYVQTE
```

0	2
14	13
23	16
6	20
70	29
14	11
27	3
12	37
4	45
19	27
36	47
8	23
40	19
13	10
8	2
29	47
80	29
27	23
7	7
2	36

Are you sure? See page 194.
Copy the decrypted text on page 197.

139

CALCULATE

REMEMBER THE ACTIVITY: archery

10 - 6 = _____	28 + 32 + 12 = _____
29 - 21 = _____	3 • 9 + 46 = _____
10 • 7 = _____	5 • 9 - 33 = _____
12 + 14 = _____	7 • 9 - 37 = _____
19 + 27 = _____	4 • 7 + 50 = _____
40 - 11 = _____	10 • 2 + 9 = _____
10 • 5 = _____	52 - 5 - 34 = _____
9 • 10 = _____	7 • 6 + 28 = _____
7 • 6 = _____	10 • 7 - 31 = _____
25 - 14 = _____	42 + 30 + 8 = _____
9 • 5 = _____	58 + 53 - 14 = _____
4 • 2 = _____	4 • 8 + 48 = _____
26 + 27 = _____	42 - 14 - 28 = _____
7 • 5 = _____	6 • 9 - 31 = _____
4 • 3 = _____	21 + 23 + 36 = _____
8 • 9 = _____	27 + 38 + 13 = _____
11 + 20 = _____	43 + 60 - 43 = _____
18 + 21 = _____	53 + 21 - 42 = _____
15 + 25 = _____	52 - 18 - 34 = _____
9 • 2 = _____	7 • 9 - 44 = _____

day 13

Additional tasks - only for math lovers!

9 - 9 = ____   5 • 3 - 13 = ____

21 - 7 = ____   29 - 13 - 3 = ____

15 + 8 = ____   3 • 9 - 11 = ____

2 • 3 = ____   7 + 18 - 5 = ____

7 • 10 = ____   3 + 9 + 17 = ____

24 - 10 = ____   26 - 11 - 4 = ____

16 + 11 = ____   26 - 13 - 10 = ____

5 + 7 = ____   18 + 22 - 3 = ____

2 • 2 = ____   6 • 10 - 15 = ____

25 - 6 = ____   5 • 2 + 17 = ____

9 • 4 = ____   9 + 26 + 12 = ____

23 - 15 = ____   23 + 28 - 28 = ____

4 • 10 = ____   3 + 8 + 8 = ____

17 - 4 = ____   25 - 3 - 12 = ____

22 - 14 = ____   25 - 4 - 19 = ____

8 + 21 = ____   19 + 8 + 20 = ____

10 • 8 = ____   27 + 20 - 18 = ____

12 + 15 = ____   8 • 6 - 25 = ____

17 - 10 = ____   4 • 4 - 9 = ____

12 - 10 = ____   26 + 18 - 8 = ____

Decrypted original text from the previous page:
DETERMINED

FIND THE NUMBERS!

4	72
8	73
70	12
26	26
46	78
29	29
50	13
90	70
42	39
11	80
45	97
8	80
53	0
35	23
12	80
72	78
31	60
39	32
40	0
18	19

Mark and count: 46

```
40984635494655364242412573446
76512086808161934821289696189
96518479638546489977469287480
14489893393238632569345738463
46738618721192730743375646997
99888246991470974646233294774
49167889585255909512435850586
35649488903635269187791340819
84909846615827448363469654627
56471148628174137760469292461
36985289295413768846787728445
41799387579217614281504691204
87588093844589578072469046813
```

Mark and count: 722

```
5404327066873182171815806101520
6551883599542311147223882028080
2997432458956111714441587067220
2442019252559053954859307225770
5191206368299633292261243138360
7229922969371301782302856937760
2258644301638156497539815291400
6915197225383579795113955212450
5357326375347392426309277861520
5918421205689616547227962054480
6669646892954702475914101972820
1876144956312303248701598858720
8993711089283793729145778953850
```

Are you sure? See page 195!

Now draw the visualized picture again with as many details as possible:

```
┌─────────────────────────────────────┐
│                                       │
│                                       │
│                                       │
│                                       │
│                                       │
│                                       │
│                                       │
│                                       │
└─────────────────────────────────────┘
```

TRY TO REMEMBER!

What should you find?

- River: _____
- Country: _____
- Decrypted text: _____

What words should you memorize?

- Object: _____
- Activity: _____

day 14

WARM UP!

REMEMBER THE OBJECT: stone

20 - 10 = _____	27 - 11 - 12 = _____
9 • 6 = _____	8 + 18 + 4 = _____
3 + 12 = _____	28 - 9 - 5 = _____
18 - 11 = _____	7 + 11 + 7 = _____
8 • 8 = _____	16 - 7 - 4 = _____
18 - 10 = _____	30 - 4 - 6 = _____
6 + 8 = _____	11 + 5 + 9 = _____
3 • 8 = _____	27 + 9 - 30 = _____
9 + 9 = _____	28 - 10 - 7 = _____
7 + 13 = _____	15 + 9 + 6 = _____
3 • 3 = _____	13 + 20 - 20 = _____
6 - 5 = _____	19 - 6 - 12 = _____
8 • 3 = _____	29 - 14 - 10 = _____
6 + 12 = _____	28 - 14 - 10 = _____
13 - 4 = _____	7 + 10 + 7 = _____
8 • 2 = _____	12 + 4 + 5 = _____
2 + 14 = _____	28 - 22 - 3 = _____
9 + 3 = _____	25 + 5 - 22 = _____
7 - 3 = _____	9 + 20 - 14 = _____
6 + 2 = _____	4 + 28 - 5 = _____

Sketch the picture as precisely as possible and memorize the details so that you can draw it again later:

WORDS AND LETTERS

10	4
54	30
15	14
7	25
64	5
8	20
14	25
24	6
18	11
20	30
9	13
1	1
24	5
18	4
9	24
16	21
16	3
12	8
4	15
8	27

Decipher the following code:

M	B	Y	H	P	V	_	Q	B	S	I	Z	L	Y
5	1	2	5	3	3	3	1	3	7	5	4	1	2
1	2	5	1	1	3	2	2	4	1	4	1	1	4

– – – – – – – – – – – – – –

– – – – – – – – – – – – – –
11 13 10 2 7 1 8 12 5 4 9 3 6 14

Original text: (turn the page)

– – – – – – – – – – – – – –
1 2 3 4 5 6 7 8 9 10 11 12 13 14

ABCDEFGHIJKLMNOPQRSTUVWXYZ_ABCDEFGHIJ

Mark and count: MEKONG

```
NKEGNGENEEOMEKONGNKGONONONKKEKOGOGG
NEKMEMNKMEKONGKGOEGEEMEKONGOONMKENG
MOOMKNMOMEKONGKNMKMEKONGNNNOMKGMOMO
GOMNOGOEENNNENEOMGOEEOKOOMEKONGGNGN
KMGEOEGGMMNMGMKMNENOGOMEKONGMMGGENK
KGMKOKOMMOMMEKONGENNEENNOMOKMNEKOEM
EMMEKONGGMONKEMNKNEEGOOEEOEKGNEKKMM
GGKKNKEEKENOGKMEKONGNGGMNKOMNGOKKGK
NKONKGGGMEMNNEMONONNKNKKGMKOOEONNON
OGMEOGNOOMEKONGGKEKOMMEKONGKKKNMMGK
EEMEKONGEMEKONGKONONMOKMMMEEKNOKMKE
EGMMOMKKMENNEONNMNGMGGOOEEOOKKMKNOG
GKEKNGEMEKONGGOMEKOEONGOOMKMNMKOMEM
```

148

Mark and count: TAIWAN

```
TAIWANNCVZFVCZKCDQEGTAIWANFNAKYDEFI
HGXWBTAIWANVECCQTBMHPUTGTAIWANDWDLJ
NXCFDDUYVFVBHLDEBEOMNBQXYEVXPORQVRB
UXXQXOKNQTAVATAIWANWXSMAWIUZAJGTWAB
TAIWANTTAIWANULKEHEUCQPITVTNKCJVJMY
EZOOYLLJKBXTAIWANUJCUUICSGTAIWANLJC
UFVDPRNBOWVXZAEZSLOEKNSBLTQGIAHLYAA
UITFOIZLGSTAIWANTYMJKTAIWANNMZLGWRJ
OQUVFGBYVTAIWANCYCZEDGXASHFCPJXXPCG
GLTSNOCEQZTAIWANWWLTVGTAIWANZDAKNNE
LAWDGCCHYIYGPWMYVMIXJOHSPHJOFTAIWAN
BOVOXQJHMXVXOGIEGGSTFRYBLVKMEFQEUKY
UCGSBGGLYARIUIDJVJQZFMTOMJKEAXXEKJA
SLEBVJILSTAIWANSLETAIWANPWKFJLHYRES
RCTGCEPXJENPVJDTJATAIWANMFNSUZNFNOM
XOJWHDEJHWVTAIWANMJXPODGALGAHKXCXWS
TAIWANBOKETAIWANJZLCORAXQBTPGTAIWAN
YZPPBLNONPPDPOXRSQYVLHDMHNPHTAIWANG
NUWWQVWQVXJGAZIOCQWVKFHMTUJYAGJDZWY
TAIWANNOJAHRGPQNJRUJTAIWANTAKAHDZQY
OVLBKJEUWMWLTTAIWANKGVLREPHPHIJUHJN
ROPQGDNUDIFISAFGFSMDTQXNUWEGABMPRTR
LSPCROUFCRUCSBHXJXIBAXTAIWANUJOAMMK
CQKHZTAIWANUZZKRZTJKTUFBMCPMMSMMFKH
SBMWQNEHIFSDUOMPTAIWANGGRSDSDBDDRTA
ATPGFWTAIWANDVLUSVKPJJDTAIWANZANAXW
QQTAIWANAWZBLFHBDDBSQJGOSTAIWANZSYJ
SHTAIWANPWYTAIWANSTODOPTAIWANTAIWAN
JOFVHQFJQOAPXXVXIDZYUCCJVUTAIWANCST
```

7	50
17	37
7	7
30	12
24	30
70	4
17	5
2	44
4	14
24	15
6	43
13	23
20	45
17	41
13	0
28	44
10	10
4	1
19	1
20	31

Are you sure? See page 194.
Copy the decrypted text on page 197.

CALCULATE

4 • 6 = _____	20 + 7 + 21 = _____
4 • 9 = _____	19 + 37 - 47 = _____
23 - 5 = _____	7 • 8 - 45 = _____
9 • 8 = _____	20 + 44 + 18 = _____
13 - 13 = _____	10 + 44 + 13 = _____
26 - 21 = _____	8 • 3 - 24 = _____
29 - 11 = _____	51 - 8 - 23 = _____
4 • 2 = _____	55 - 6 - 18 = _____
13 + 7 = _____	9 • 2 - 18 = _____
25 - 20 = _____	3 • 7 + 12 = _____
13 - 12 = _____	43 + 55 - 50 = _____
34 - 34 = _____	4 • 6 + 40 = _____
30 + 22 = _____	49 + 14 + 30 = _____
7 + 9 = _____	9 • 9 - 27 = _____
30 + 8 = _____	55 + 36 - 60 = _____
6 + 27 = _____	7 • 10 - 26 = _____
15 + 14 = _____	3 • 6 - 6 = _____
24 - 6 = _____	19 + 26 + 47 = _____
5 • 2 = _____	8 • 4 + 42 = _____
30 - 30 = _____	37 - 13 - 13 = _____

Additional tasks - only for math lovers!

11 - 4 = ____	19 + 3 + 28 = ____
7 + 10 = ____	4 • 3 + 25 = ____
29 - 22 = ____	24 + 4 - 21 = ____
7 + 23 = ____	30 - 4 - 14 = ____
6 • 4 = ____	16 + 8 + 6 = ____
7 • 10 = ____	24 - 16 - 4 = ____
11 + 6 = ____	25 - 10 - 10 = ____
21 - 19 = ____	22 + 15 + 7 = ____
16 - 12 = ____	16 + 23 - 25 = ____
29 - 5 = ____	24 + 4 - 13 = ____
17 - 11 = ____	14 + 25 + 4 = ____
6 + 7 = ____	9 • 3 - 4 = ____
4 • 5 = ____	16 + 10 + 19 = ____
22 - 5 = ____	3 + 16 + 22 = ____
8 + 5 = ____	10 - 6 - 4 = ____
6 + 22 = ____	26 + 5 + 13 = ____
27 - 17 = ____	5 • 7 - 25 = ____
2 • 2 = ____	16 - 9 - 6 = ____
26 - 7 = ____	19 - 13 - 5 = ____
10 • 2 = ____	5 • 2 + 21 = ____

Decrypted original text from the previous page:
AND INTERESTED

FIND THE NUMBERS!

24	48
36	9
18	11
72	82
0	67
5	0
18	20
8	31
20	0
5	33
1	48
0	64
52	93
16	54
38	31
33	44
29	12
18	92
10	74
0	11

Mark and count: 13

```
16973313628390552115933 6673114
69119756814945988861836446111
12937082782395813585383 2678846
71821322998927583758152 9957124
18423471631397226097141 7507869
36147522709684758463247 0136583
17212512716781628539839 7269940
83703282754375345865854 7134589
39534513603249244945227 6919014
65902783482528522747601 8381325
55731313901530211139584 9139917
93368012954460284877948 4469274
72447295319534735677532 3283254
```

Mark and count: 694

```
67520926714860636165898 3273514
37224825111797945544369 4730999
69472169469453074329280 3993227
69440553148526956444112 8253464
62714790735269490614024 0600382
60378076568267233745956 8724552
80838188550740050259060 1600283
56797916024116531978732 1572349
77494323629780099231778 7135539
31277923021468476374993 9694694
23838569438245969477286 9246771
67846629478514840114969 2457185
24941648954020082522469 4229511
```

Are you sure? See page 195!

REMEMBER!

Now draw the visualized picture again with as many details as possible:

TRY TO REMEMBER!

What should you find?

- River: _____
- Country: _____
- Decrypted text: _____

What words should you memorize?

- Object: _____
- Activity: _____

day 15

WARM UP!

REMEMBER THE OBJECT: tires

18 - 11 = _____	7 + 5 + 6 = _____
6 • 9 = _____	12 + 5 + 5 = _____
20 - 15 = _____	29 - 18 - 10 = _____
19 - 19 = _____	22 + 4 + 4 = _____
9 • 9 = _____	4 + 12 + 14 = _____
15 + 2 = _____	5 + 27 - 8 = _____
5 • 5 = _____	23 - 9 - 12 = _____
9 - 2 = _____	4 + 14 + 12 = _____
20 - 11 = _____	26 - 8 - 9 = _____
14 - 10 = _____	6 + 4 + 17 = _____
12 - 2 = _____	27 - 8 - 8 = _____
5 + 3 = _____	15 - 11 - 4 = _____
8 - 3 = _____	30 - 3 - 26 = _____
2 • 7 = _____	9 + 6 + 4 = _____
4 • 10 = _____	21 - 5 - 13 = _____
12 + 4 = _____	22 - 18 - 4 = _____
9 + 3 = _____	12 + 7 + 7 = _____
2 • 9 = _____	9 + 4 + 4 = _____
9 • 4 = _____	4 + 4 + 5 = _____
18 - 4 = _____	20 + 27 - 24 = _____

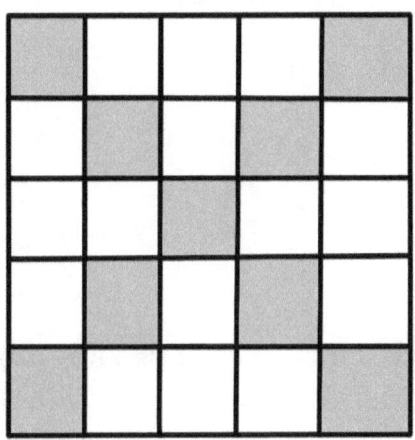

Sketch the picture as precisely as possible and memorize the details so that you can draw it again later:

7	18
54	22
5	1
0	30
81	30
17	24
25	2
7	30
9	9
4	27
10	11
8	0
5	1
14	19
40	3
16	0
12	26
18	17
36	13
14	23

Decipher the following code:

```
T N _ I P G H
5 1 2 5 7 4 1
2 6 7 4 2 3 6

_ _ _ _ _ _ _
_ _ _ _ _ _ _
3 6 1 7 4 2 5
```

Original text: (turn the page)
```
_ _ _ _ _ _ _
1 2 3 4 5 6 7
```

ABCDEFGHIJKLMNOPQRSTUVWXYZ_ABCDEFGHIJ

Mark and count: YANGTZE

```
YEYAANYANGTZEZEYGETYZGYANGTZEYGGGZY
ATNGZZNYNNGNYGZGNYYZEYETYANGTZEGYYT
ZEGETZZZGNYYZEGZEYANGTZETYANGTZEZZZ
GZAGZZEGZGYANGTZEYANGTZEAEZNNENGGAA
ZNZTYGEGGAYAYNTAGEGEYANGTZEZYANGTZE
ANTAYNEYNNGEZENTYANGTZEYNYYZZTYGZEE
EGZYYENNYNGYZEGATNATTZZZGEYETZYAEEE
YANGTZENGGTYTYANGTZEGYAEANZZEYNEAZA
GAYANGTZEGEGYANGTZEAGTTNGYANGTZENGA
AYEYYANGTZEAYANGTZEATNNNYZGTZZAAZAG
YANGTZEZGYYAZENYAETZTNZGEEZEYNTNYZN
YANGTZENETGYTGTENNETYZNZTGZGEZAEGNA
ZYGYGAYANGTZEYTYANGTZEZGTNTAETZATAY
```

Mark and count: KOREA

```
RTOWWZOYTVSXFHANKOREANCQDFXSBJAKPJM
XRKZKOREAWJMVGGHHLKOREAKOREAAYSPWRG
XUQIVPXLDYJKOREABXKOREAQQGQCAHNTFXT
PDRVWYRLZZNQKOREALKZBYUWUKOREAUIYMR
NBMOMOKOREAEKOREAQSYYTWGGHYIRKOREAM
BMSKOREAPLQUYVBAXDOSGZDKOREABHCHOPF
DUOFKOREABKOREAKOREAAUBKAYKOREAENDB
GKGSKOREAXSJKEDQBKOREAAZAAZOCXDJOPC
BJEVPSHKOREAUWRKRJYXDWUKDPPUZTICVCN
BVIGTFKOREARMURCPRBVDRGDXJAGOZNVIBF
NFHMWJQPRFGSTVGCHTTNOYBPZPAHRRURSLO
TRZKOREAKOREARXYHQWCVGFZHLYKOREANUP
QKOREAMRKDIJZKNGBUXLIJEYKOREAUSBUAI
BEGVRKOREACHZLUDAXWKYZELLPMKZBVVVJF
HJFNKOREAPERGZEICNJOVWDBALCYNKOREAF
ZHROHBUQGHSJMYFQJXRYLYAZQBSEDTOSRMS
KOREAILKOREAVBYYOESHPHZMLQVFKOREADS
OMNDXVXOEAQPUKOREALCPMQEKOREAJIATOC
CPIIOJEXBGFUMHBKQSOATJAIDCAAVDZJDLI
MVXEZRPSQWKOZPKOREACAMFAHTWXTGBNQPV
LCVMKDXGUKOREAGFMGOXCZZFEKOREAHCUMX
JLKOREAKOREAUTHYIVORTGZXQFIVKOREATG
GCJQXHKIOMOWPFKDIXVPXDYKOREAUOKOREA
EKLOBYCGBZZEWVBGBFGKOREABSTIFSISYSY
KOREAINBNIIHAFPODDIZOBNVOZARRGQKZNP
JYYBRMIEUMZZTUOFIDZUXWYAWDKOREABEJK
HBEUUZEXOKKOREANYTQFPEOALHCMDICAEUM
EEGNTTLJNPOSUMXOVYRYMKDIXEPPRWMAJXX
NRGMTWALWQKXWOAAJNEXBKOREAWQWHKOREA
```

16	46
2	11
21	21
80	2
26	36
13	0
25	17
54	10
17	35
29	23
20	13
18	41
12	16
60	40
10	39
26	0
5	30
28	3
29	8
6	4

Are you sure? See page 194.
Copy the decrypted text on page 197.

CALCULATE

REMEMBER THE ACTIVITY: dancing

28 - 21 = ____	10 • 3 + 41 = ____
3 • 5 = ____	8 • 6 - 23 = ____
20 - 5 = ____	52 - 4 - 22 = ____
9 • 2 = ____	6 • 8 + 44 = ____
30 + 14 = ____	10 • 2 + 47 = ____
33 - 23 = ____	15 + 18 - 24 = ____
30 - 19 = ____	15 - 4 - 7 = ____
31 - 31 = ____	8 • 6 + 11 = ____
20 + 23 = ____	3 • 10 + 58 = ____
33 - 14 = ____	7 • 10 - 56 = ____
4 • 3 = ____	10 • 5 - 34 = ____
29 - 28 = ____	4 • 4 + 49 = ____
28 + 21 = ____	18 + 16 + 57 = ____
7 • 7 = ____	8 • 7 - 14 = ____
14 - 11 = ____	26 + 20 + 23 = ____
12 - 12 = ____	7 • 5 + 46 = ____
2 • 5 = ____	45 - 4 - 12 = ____
3 • 7 = ____	10 • 6 - 54 = ____
2 • 10 = ____	4 • 10 + 35 = ____
6 + 8 = ____	52 - 25 - 21 = ____

Additional tasks - only for math lovers!

25 - 9 = _____	3 • 6 + 28 = _____
30 - 28 = _____	28 - 8 - 9 = _____
14 + 7 = _____	27 + 14 - 20 = _____
10 • 8 = _____	25 - 8 - 15 = _____
14 + 12 = _____	8 • 2 + 20 = _____
26 - 13 = _____	29 - 15 - 14 = _____
18 + 7 = _____	9 + 22 - 14 = _____
6 • 9 = _____	28 - 5 - 13 = _____
21 - 4 = _____	15 + 23 - 3 = _____
6 + 23 = _____	13 + 3 + 7 = _____
12 + 8 = _____	28 - 11 - 4 = _____
3 • 6 = _____	5 + 25 + 11 = _____
6 • 2 = _____	4 • 3 + 4 = _____
10 • 6 = _____	21 + 15 + 4 = _____
30 - 20 = _____	9 • 4 + 3 = _____
10 + 16 = _____	9 - 4 - 5 = _____
22 - 17 = _____	5 • 4 + 10 = _____
23 + 5 = _____	25 - 18 - 4 = _____
7 + 22 = _____	5 • 6 - 22 = _____
21 - 15 = _____	28 - 19 - 5 = _____

Decrypted original text from the previous page:
IN YOUR

FIND THE NUMBERS!

7	71
15	25
15	26
18	92
44	67
10	9
11	4
0	59
43	88
19	14
12	16
1	65
49	91
49	42
3	69
0	81
10	29
21	6
20	75
14	6

Mark and count: 37

```
95889065422867169628372254 9920
19253724767126198956192037 6820
87982742856021226263816937 3659
86814263823125373584749924 1158
77812967206844503798343168 8254
20378099711447669922187537 5425
85761937214683488160909821 3758
31792516371483272328557761 4338
23136837171865879259449643 3761
44709198444688144352228760 4011
75701226729331503883229315 7023
22342141472580424975371082 2461
66223741495148376833379915 7558
```

Mark and count: 256

```
46053328167780631644028551 5774
83173578862695955986473134 0488
68222220473927463539145315 3804
78328631415119627614257561 7997
27629817831465099775160154 0256
25687679195232238314925652 7856
30125648937125698752177896 4256
19736183093644725638663624 4332
31133361924870685339396477 2256
73998159462811983475371619 9234
52983458116184165967720599 4295
98582188625667516567629998 0256
18353461634347970330447746 9317
```

Are you sure? See page 195!

REMEMBER!

Now draw the visualized picture again with as many details as possible:

TRY TO REMEMBER!

What should you find?

- River: _____
- Country: _____
- Decrypted text: _____

What words should you memorize?

- Object: _____
- Activity: _____

163

day 16

WARM UP!

REMEMBER THE OBJECT: braclet

2 • 2 = _____	6 + 15 - 17 = _____
8 - 2 = _____	9 + 5 + 14 = _____
3 + 14 = _____	30 - 12 - 8 = _____
9 + 11 = _____	29 - 19 - 8 = _____
13 - 3 = _____	14 + 6 - 5 = _____
7 - 2 = _____	7 + 16 - 15 = _____
18 - 6 = _____	19 + 5 + 6 = _____
20 - 2 = _____	17 + 6 + 5 = _____
6 + 3 = _____	6 + 8 + 12 = _____
10 + 8 = _____	7 + 18 - 8 = _____
6 • 6 = _____	9 + 4 + 10 = _____
7 - 7 = _____	10 + 8 + 10 = _____
10 + 3 = _____	23 + 4 - 24 = _____
2 • 7 = _____	17 - 11 - 6 = _____
3 + 12 = _____	27 - 4 - 7 = _____
4 + 12 = _____	4 + 9 + 5 = _____
13 + 7 = _____	5 + 7 + 13 = _____
2 • 10 = _____	29 - 7 - 12 = _____
16 - 9 = _____	13 + 9 - 15 = _____
9 • 7 = _____	27 - 13 - 10 = _____

Sketch the picture as precisely as possible and memorize the details so that you can draw it again later:

4	4
6	28
17	10
20	2
10	15
5	8
12	30
18	28
9	26
18	17
36	23
0	28
13	3
14	0
15	16
16	18
20	25
20	10
7	7
63	4

```
Decipher the following code:

W J Q U M N _
6 2 1 5 6 1 2
3 7 1 4 2 4 1

_ _ _ _ _ _ _
_ _ _ _ _ _ _
5 7 6 4 2 1 3

Original text: (turn the page)
_ _ _ _ _ _ _
1 2 3 4 5 6 7

ABCDEFGHIJKLMNOPQRSTUVWXYZ_ABCDEFGHIJ
```

Mark and count: SHANNON

```
SOHNNSNNSONNSNOOOHONNSASHANNONNNNAA
NNSHANNONSNNSHSNNNNANNAOANSNSHANNON
NASSHANNONAASNNANNSHANNONANNHNNASON
NOSANNNNNNNNNANNANHNSSANNHSHANNONN
NNNNNNASHANNONHHNHSNNSHANNNNASOSHAS
HNNOSHANNONSNNHHNSHANNONNNNHNSHNNNS
HANAHHAHNANSHANNONNONOAANNNNONNNNHA
SNANSHANNONNNONANHHHHAHNHASHANNONHO
NONOSHANNONNNOSNSHANNONNSNNANNAOSNO
HSSNSSOASANOANOSHANNONNOSHANNONANHO
SHANNONAOANAANNOHASNSASHANNONOOOANSA
NNOSHANNONNNAANONNNANOONNNSHANNONHA
OSOAANOHNNSSNHSHSHANNONNHNONSHANNON
```

Mark and count: INDIA

```
CROVTGINDIAJDPMFINDIAHZCOQSJCCXIYXP
CQVWNCVJDBVMINDIAMKIZXQUCBJEEQUSIBZ
JDRXBRXBIEWPSWYCKTINDIAWAYJIAQBRCPI
XTSHUPTCAGSBHWKYDIACPUTKWCBDGFUVORX
SKKIINDIACRPVWBSKUKMTRRINDIADGHZUMD
OEELKEJLINDIAVBDXOVLRHINDIAKJQNXYRO
FGAALTSINDIAAGZPZXYHXKXDINDIAINDIAR
RKOINDIAINDIAJNVUQINDIAUXZAINDIADIX
FHEPOYXSKTXHCZINDIAMOULIOUULQUSEGED
NJUSYIUAYDPCTRZQOPNICKKRBYIUGAGCSNR
WINDIACEKKDTIJRFYDZBVMTNWCDDMDFFPWV
DGWZDDRPZPZBRVZBALOKNUHEEJDZKUZDDJN
INDIACSZQTULAOQOFRCRCOXSIHWHECGXRUW
CXNZDHWRRZFGGULDOINDIAEDKPSVNHMQJTO
CUIORQFZUFFGBGHULINDIAMVEURWZOZEXNU
DTVPKNHUGUTINDIAFKOPJZTCBINDIARFQDK
QRHQSTBGBQJUYAIFDHLBXYGFENNXEEINDIA
QXJDHZRQJXPBEGSQUTLGXNTCINDIANHAHCJ
RINDIAZMINDIAZJUQKADEDRIWFLNZCNVASS
FAUSQBNTIINDIAIGFGCQPPREXTOFJLPIMRY
ZGYEKNOBVQYYUXBMDTQZHRUBMXHLSNGYAQN
MUNAFAVTISTBHPXDEPMAPNUZJRWKTAIWGBN
EHKQNLJQINDIALMFDINDIADWXXVYFBPJDLO
LIPYTJHGNMNURLAINDIALHUMINDIAMHLHUY
INDIAZYJLWJINDIADJPNSSFFMIWZADIHNTB
FZLGINDIAOZKGFFMRBAKWRISQHEIEOVHTVD
VWGGKINDIAZKPXIWVMUGQVHJEBGINDIAYGN
WLYJGBRLNYXFINDIAINDIAKXHINDIATCDUD
INDIAEAQPHXXAZMWZIOMLZXCAIOZQFHXQEY
```

6	48
26	45
3	0
14	34
12	3
0	42
20	31
24	35
12	45
18	6
30	25
16	24
15	8
22	10
20	11
42	18
14	15
50	30
20	13
15	19

Are you sure? See page 194.
Copy the decrypted text on page 197.

CALCULATE

REMEMBER THE ACTIVITY: golf

$10 \cdot 8 =$ _____ $36 - 8 - 8 =$ _____

$6 \cdot 5 =$ _____ $21 + 15 - 36 =$ _____

$21 + 19 =$ _____ $9 \cdot 4 - 29 =$ _____

$16 - 13 =$ _____ $30 + 31 + 31 =$ _____

$39 - 14 =$ _____ $59 - 19 - 21 =$ _____

$28 + 17 =$ _____ $6 + 10 + 13 =$ _____

$35 - 20 =$ _____ $10 \cdot 8 - 37 =$ _____

$27 + 17 =$ _____ $46 + 46 - 18 =$ _____

$34 - 19 =$ _____ $44 - 16 - 16 =$ _____

$15 + 6 =$ _____ $9 \cdot 7 + 26 =$ _____

$7 \cdot 5 =$ _____ $60 - 15 - 12 =$ _____

$10 - 8 =$ _____ $9 \cdot 7 + 32 =$ _____

$8 \cdot 2 =$ _____ $12 + 35 + 28 =$ _____

$24 - 22 =$ _____ $16 + 56 - 53 =$ _____

$11 - 9 =$ _____ $16 + 56 - 13 =$ _____

$22 - 17 =$ _____ $19 + 51 + 9 =$ _____

$18 + 7 =$ _____ $56 - 19 - 21 =$ _____

$39 - 27 =$ _____ $2 \cdot 7 + 18 =$ _____

$4 \cdot 3 =$ _____ $18 + 28 + 26 =$ _____

$24 + 11 =$ _____ $10 \cdot 8 - 26 =$ _____

day 16

Additional tasks - only for math lovers!

2 • 3 = ____

7 + 19 = ____

12 - 9 = ____

7 + 7 = ____

2 • 6 = ____

30 - 30 = ____

5 • 4 = ____

14 + 10 = ____

26 - 14 = ____

6 • 3 = ____

12 + 18 = ____

4 • 4 = ____

25 - 10 = ____

30 - 8 = ____

2 • 10 = ____

6 • 7 = ____

20 - 6 = ____

5 • 10 = ____

7 + 13 = ____

3 • 5 = ____

27 + 7 + 14 = ____

29 + 9 + 7 = ____

16 + 14 - 30 = ____

18 + 11 + 5 = ____

20 - 6 - 11 = ____

6 • 4 + 18 = ____

4 • 4 + 15 = ____

8 • 3 + 11 = ____

7 • 3 + 24 = ____

28 - 12 - 10 = ____

7 • 6 - 17 = ____

7 • 7 - 25 = ____

26 - 10 - 8 = ____

28 - 15 - 3 = ____

29 - 6 - 12 = ____

8 • 6 - 30 = ____

2 • 9 - 3 = ____

7 • 2 + 16 = ____

30 - 4 - 13 = ____

6 + 5 + 8 = ____

Decrypted original text from the previous page:
SUCCESS

FIND THE NUMBERS!

80	20
30	0
40	7
3	92
25	19
45	29
15	43
44	74
15	12
21	89
35	33
2	95
16	75
2	19
2	59
5	79
25	16
12	32
12	72
35	54

Mark and count: 76

```
88935376901135632836762631592 8
61763176839584888476684677171 2
16101410978176865161466876938 8
60735047979117321686517378796 3
75507676919522761776516514567 6
99575341334676267561241276582 0
21411115205330912563361766238 9
76799869833148272729379568165 5
26886578289346384160825185428 2
69367676115895426910821178764 5
67358539897341742682833486938 7
83279638172776761498426134408 0
27726983666638322977591327184 2
```

Mark and count: 982

```
18398297068878372771026581758 8
37383450046056471841675695045 0
91633286519582461737837698217 6
60035138519274225873348340129 5
44229919823010835492871095123 2
27311263117438661679540954391 9
61823035319049654515379572959 4
87342977023691438963142685878 1
55357098254259386271829942345 5
15964536675318924779398287764 2
71444178448292451180480577021 5
14078711825720164174917277377 0
51150318931041699134791072720 9
```

172   Are you sure? See page 195!

Now draw the visualized picture again with as many details as possible:

```

```

TRY TO REMEMBER!

What should you find?

- River: _____
- Country: _____
- Decrypted text: _____

What words should you memorize?

- Object: _____
- Activity: _____

day 17

WARM UP!

REMEMBER THE OBJECT: clock

19 - 11 = _____	4 + 17 + 8 = _____
15 - 2 = _____	14 + 12 - 21 = _____
7 - 5 = _____	16 + 20 - 10 = _____
15 - 4 = _____	19 - 11 - 6 = _____
5 + 9 = _____	27 - 6 - 16 = _____
19 - 16 = _____	4 + 10 + 8 = _____
4 • 9 = _____	6 + 8 + 4 = _____
7 • 10 = _____	27 - 6 - 3 = _____
10 - 7 = _____	4 + 11 + 11 = _____
12 - 2 = _____	23 + 16 - 11 = _____
6 • 10 = _____	16 + 7 - 9 = _____
7 - 2 = _____	4 + 11 + 5 = _____
16 - 6 = _____	13 + 4 + 5 = _____
5 • 2 = _____	7 + 7 + 10 = _____
5 + 14 = _____	30 - 6 - 13 = _____
14 - 14 = _____	15 + 25 - 29 = _____
6 • 2 = _____	15 + 17 - 19 = _____
3 + 16 = _____	26 + 15 - 26 = _____
9 • 9 = _____	29 - 9 - 5 = _____
5 • 5 = _____	4 + 7 + 6 = _____

Sketch the picture as precisely as possible and memorize the details so that you can draw it again later:

WORDS AND LETTERS

8	29
13	5
2	26
11	2
14	5
3	22
36	18
70	18
3	26
10	28
60	14
5	20
10	22
10	24
19	11
0	11
12	13
19	15
81	15
25	17

```
Decipher the following code:

L X H W P S W J S
3 1 4 5 3 7 4 6 5
6 2 3 4 6 1 1 2 4

_ _ _ _ _ _ _ _ _
_ _ _ _ _ _ _ _ _
3 4 2 7 1 8 5 6 9

Original text: (turn the page)
_ _ _ _ _ _ _ _ _
1 2 3 4 5 6 7 8 9

ABCDEFGHIJKLMNOPQRSTUVWXYZ_ABCDEFGHIJ
```

Mark and count: YUKON

```
OYOKNYNNUUYNKOKYUUUYYUKONUNYYNKOKKU
NONNYUKYOUNYYNKKOOKUOUKOYYYOOUNOKKY
KONONNKUNUYKONUYUUUOKUKYOOYUKONKNUY
NUONKUYKYKONYKUKYUUKYUKONKNYUNYUOUY
KYOYOUYUKONYNKUUKUYUKONYOOYKOYUKNKU
KYUKONYUYKKNYUKONUYNKNUYYYUKONNKYUO
OOKOYOUOUKUUOYOOYUKONNKNKNONUOOYNOU
YYUKONONKYUKONYKOONOKNKYONOKYYNUUNU
UKONOYUKONUKOOYYUKONOKKYYKOYUOONNNO
KNOYKUUONUNYUNKUNUUKYUKKNOOKOUYKOOO
NYYUKONUKKYYKOYUKONYUOKOYNOYOYYYUOO
UOYNYUKONUUNNKYUKONYUNYYNYKOUNUNOKO
KNOYUOUYUUYUNKNNYUKONUOKYKUKUYUKONK
```

Mark and count: AUSTRALIA

```
GFEERORICJWNROXLOCTNECHSVWEIMLAHHVJ
FOWOTDEAQJBNZADQKACNESVYLMOUDCYRJBL
TVBJZGWCEDVFTVCYTAUSTRALIAJFPCJDATR
IKKDQLWKYAUSTRALIAHXXXBPLMJSZXCOGLL
AMPQAUSTRALIAAUSTRALIARAUSTRALIACPJ
RYQHHMJCFMBUPYXFVAUSTRALIAREGAZVOGS
EGRIIYJGAIAJHSJZPUNFFWEMKUEXGZIFDTB
AZYEZRHHPWYGZEUGNHLMVLLACANPYUJBLGI
XFEOIWJRXSNYMYWPMZKPVEADCESLELSHHYL
UTDBWOCGMKCEIGJMBAUSTRALIAUICUHDTGK
ZJTKHSRGUAOIYOJJWZWFHJKFMAVCYDNNARB
UINNUHRESNRKIKCDOHFUAFWPAUSTRALIAQA
QXQUTVMZUEBPREKMNIFXZAWEEJEBLCDPFSQ
GGOXIRSTUKMYQZHEUYAUSTRALIABEQBVYVZ
KAUSTRALIAZBLYHWMOABASFOUVGFFGBCCLX
PYHNJVMTYKRAUSTRALIAWZOQAUSTRALIAGL
TPREAUSTRALIAIVHVNCTRVLRJUSPCGTQOYK
MUDJVVNDJVWEMMHZYXAUSTRALIAMLVSXUVT
QEJPSWYRUIRCTNQSOSWIKEOPAUSTRALIAMW
KNOVGOHNMJBCJYAUSTRALIAXQFKNAORAJCZ
KTMLLAUSTRALIAEGUEBHYAUSTRALIAOVZTQ
ELGDIEJXCGENVKMTCWJAUSTRALIASNHUQEY
MRDWCVSTMIAUSTRALIAEPBOLQIFZTTHUWJT
LEFAUSTRALIAYHDPKZEXKKDEKCUQRNEXCZP
YZGVWWHLKLMCWTNFNSVAUSTRALIAUQUGHAC
EAUSTRALIAMWIOJGCGEFJIUUBSOXLTKODEZ
HPZUJAZAUSTRALIAMRMRIZRRISOCKSIBWCK
FSCUGVQTQKOUKFOSGBVSPNHKMBGOOPVJYVC
AUSTRALIAHYSGMRKMEMICLSXEAUSTRALIAJ
```

7	25
10	17
10	0
26	27
28	24
30	32
23	36
90	2
23	41
27	21
19	36
20	27
3	33
7	43
30	42
22	17
30	34
2	36
21	37
21	28

Are you sure? See page 194.
Copy the decrypted text on page 197.

CALCULATE

REMEMBER THE ACTIVITY: volleyball

27 + 15 = _____	17 + 56 + 19 = _____
18 + 10 = _____	42 + 18 - 25 = _____
25 - 5 = _____	45 + 16 + 17 = _____
11 + 18 = _____	43 - 5 - 11 = _____
4 • 6 = _____	7 • 7 - 9 = _____
10 • 4 = _____	53 - 23 - 21 = _____
16 - 16 = _____	19 + 50 - 28 = _____
7 • 6 = _____	50 - 33 - 6 = _____
7 • 7 = _____	45 - 30 - 8 = _____
4 • 7 = _____	60 + 42 - 32 = _____
15 - 7 = _____	44 - 17 - 26 = _____
22 - 16 = _____	15 + 10 + 44 = _____
31 - 6 = _____	9 + 22 - 17 = _____
16 + 13 = _____	2 • 8 + 58 = _____
20 + 12 = _____	17 + 35 + 43 = _____
9 • 7 = _____	23 + 25 - 19 = _____
13 + 6 = _____	6 • 6 + 16 = _____
22 - 7 = _____	51 + 60 - 48 = _____
17 + 14 = _____	8 • 7 + 10 = _____
11 - 5 = _____	32 + 23 + 26 = _____

day 17

Additional tasks - only for math lovers!

18 - 11 = ____	3 + 4 + 18 = ____
5 • 2 = ____	17 + 15 - 15 = ____
21 - 11 = ____	28 - 16 - 12 = ____
19 + 7 = ____	7 • 8 - 29 = ____
16 + 12 = ____	16 + 17 - 9 = ____
6 • 5 = ____	6 • 9 - 22 = ____
7 + 16 = ____	14 + 14 + 8 = ____
9 • 10 = ____	3 • 5 - 13 = ____
28 - 5 = ____	29 + 9 + 3 = ____
3 • 9 = ____	29 - 5 - 3 = ____
23 - 4 = ____	4 • 5 + 16 = ____
2 • 10 = ____	3 + 9 + 15 = ____
26 - 23 = ____	21 + 9 + 3 = ____
14 - 7 = ____	18 + 14 + 11 = ____
14 + 16 = ____	8 • 3 + 18 = ____
11 + 11 = ____	2 • 2 + 13 = ____
5 • 6 = ____	8 • 7 - 22 = ____
7 - 5 = ____	7 • 7 - 13 = ____
3 • 7 = ____	8 + 19 + 10 = ____
10 + 11 = ____	6 • 2 + 16 = ____

Decrypted original text from the previous page:
YOU ARE A

FIND THE NUMBERS!

42	92
28	35
20	78
29	27
24	40
40	9
0	41
42	11
49	7
28	70
8	1
6	69
25	14
29	74
32	95
63	29
19	52
15	63
31	66
6	81

Mark and count: 52

64179546909693321777524265 9714
65792281194054958319764669 6952
63273229997053489717395286 4065
79468412646734601340541910 4053
69273552757150302440166173 5297
33116091177973526757284133 1028
63377452711781538970276994 6969
22624745813010476334361016 3633
81699228389443521152742411 1452
14912927795023652231778263 3299
75697376244452544817664066 5852
74684716795956358552145736 1491
17987336516189651014527611 1628

Mark and count: 846

90884630573442659687784615 5235
57821943888684648164157711 6685
93974324238784611564928422 8666
84639813843334485926159284 6886
86020620298846855152388548 777
10522328663977346676010957 5373
24167955161335829598732065 8419
69656051255420769184022484 6661
11415691421538468784669318 7797
48931845512089840228096610 2922
26320496460095710859636878 3823
58755610978269039786113794 9149
88750724166970516132495713 6618

Are you sure? See page 195!

Now draw the visualized picture again with as many details as possible:

___

TRY TO REMEMBER!

What should you find?

- River: _____
- Country: _____
- Decrypted text: _____

What words should you memorize?

- Object: _____
- Activity: _____

day 18

WARM UP!

REMEMBER THE OBJECT: box

$7 \cdot 6 =$ _____ $13 + 26 - 27 =$ _____

$8 \cdot 3 =$ _____ $22 - 3 - 3 =$ _____

$20 - 10 =$ _____ $14 + 14 - 24 =$ _____

$11 + 5 =$ _____ $13 + 18 - 27 =$ _____

$6 + 6 =$ _____ $25 + 5 - 28 =$ _____

$9 \cdot 7 =$ _____ $29 - 13 - 5 =$ _____

$5 + 9 =$ _____ $23 - 11 - 12 =$ _____

$20 - 18 =$ _____ $17 + 17 - 15 =$ _____

$4 + 7 =$ _____ $25 - 10 - 10 =$ _____

$16 + 2 =$ _____ $29 - 9 - 6 =$ _____

$2 \cdot 2 =$ _____ $21 - 3 - 9 =$ _____

$2 + 7 =$ _____ $25 - 6 - 11 =$ _____

$8 \cdot 2 =$ _____ $26 - 10 - 3 =$ _____

$16 - 7 =$ _____ $15 + 16 - 4 =$ _____

$2 \cdot 9 =$ _____ $5 + 11 + 8 =$ _____

$11 + 4 =$ _____ $19 + 10 - 10 =$ _____

$14 + 4 =$ _____ $21 + 19 - 28 =$ _____

$17 - 14 =$ _____ $24 - 17 - 4 =$ _____

$6 + 11 =$ _____ $17 - 5 - 7 =$ _____

$19 - 3 =$ _____ $5 + 19 - 14 =$ _____

Sketch the picture as precisely as possible and memorize the details so that you can draw it again later:

42	12
24	16
10	4
16	4
12	2
63	11
14	0
2	19
11	5
18	14
4	9
9	8
16	13
9	27
18	24
15	19
18	12
3	3
17	5
16	10

```
Decipher the following code:

W V Y J H K J I B L L T
7 1 6 3 5 3 1 6 1 1 1 6
2 4 1 6 1 6 7 3 4 2 3 2

– – – – – – – – – – – –

– – – – – – – – – – – –
8 6 3 10 12 5 9 2 1 11 7 4

Original text: (turn the page)

– – – – – – – – – – – –
1  2  3  4  5  6  7  8  9  10 11 12

ABCDEFGHIJKLMNOPQRSTUVWXYZ_ABCDEFGHIJ
```

Mark and count: AMUR

```
RMUAMURAARUAAMURRARAUAMURMRMMRAURAR
UURAMUAUUAMURMMUAUMRMURAMMURMRURAAM
AMURAAUURMAMURRMAMURUMRUUMAAMUUUAUU
RUUMARMMRRMAURMUUUUUUUMUUAMURRURUR
RAMURMUUMMAURAUAAAUAMUAMURAUAMURARA
UAUMRAUAMURRAUMUUMMAARARUARAMURAUU
RMUUMURRRAMMRUAAMRRAAAUMUUAMURMRRUR
RMARAMUUAUAAMURAMURAURRUAUAUARAAUMA
RAAAAMRRAMARMMUURUAAMARRUAUUAUMMUUM
UAMRURRRAMURMUAAMURMAMURUMRMAMURRUA
MRAMURAURAUAAMURUAARMRARRMRRMRUAMMU
AURURAMRUAAMUURAUUUUMRRMUMAAAARAMUA
MAAMURUARMRAMURUAAMURRMMRURURRMMMMR
```

Mark and count: ITALY

```
UJNBRATQACYOEOVMGYCCXZSLXSFITALYZHG
IZKLOXKMHLTWXGJADRLFBSFWLLCRIRYHBYY
CITALYTJWWGOVUNVXLITALYKEQYLZFUXVOY
ITALYKIITALYMIBSFHITALYHRHITALYYUNE
WSCUHHNBEXBEBSDIIITXBUFLXHAWITALYSJ
XITALYJTLXNBOZDPMITALYJMITALYITALYG
ZLTLMRITALYIQJSKORQQGZINGSUDTPZMUAS
CZITALYLDFDEITALYITALYWVLGLWLCCFSTA
CNJQGCSMNJGXVVSNVWUIUUFITALYQJDNOCT
AITALYITALYITALYWXITALYNBMBIIYDSQXL
WZZGTKSLTCZLDRUITALYPGQDBVFHNMOHFOW
UITALYBGGTULITALYPDJZJJAEOZITALYFZU
QDFYIVGLYPNEDYNQITALYHLUITALYRCMVOW
RITALYZITALYHITALYCNORBERLLIEYHSTOX
SITALYRLADKYXPEIIFEWTISYFHVWECITALY
VDCRVQOUKUMKJITALYNKKOITALYLIVHEMPO
ITALYMXINZFHOLKZBDEITALYLZZNEBFWIWR
TITALYJWVVCKUFRDOHITCNQNXQXYKLAVCEL
HDLITALYITALYSJOITALYTWLHXOWJLWVBYF
JXQIUIFIREQPRQNDFITALYYDNUQVCSMXGMW
ZMTONLITALYQXAWRJVRXTITALYXMDODQXDH
EXVHOFDBXJITALYVTGVNMMQUFPGAGYNDHFG
VZFITALYYWRYVAAUMUKFEICJCVFVITALYWG
JBITALYFMEFDLORAPITALYSEHVDRBQLPLGP
ZTQXRXJGEOLAOOHQFITALYSNIGITALYLCXX
JWAITALYWAXMBMTWMHLJITALYYMZNQYIXXS
YLAVFWCUJYABLAEPROWQLJVKDKJDFXJPDXD
ZZKLRSRUNBXRZITALYJYHDTTEDPGPBOXXLX
LWQZOWKKVXITALYJZHSRCEIPVBEBISBAHIK
```

72	33
22	45
5	21
20	9
22	49
4	50
16	38
28	50
0	33
4	4
14	48
25	6
40	4
1	33
70	16
9	7
27	10
70	3
45	1
12	4

Are you sure? See page 194.
Copy the decrypted text on page 197.

CALCULATE

REMEMBER THE ACTIVITY: canoeing

38 - 20 = ____	47 - 14 - 7 = ____
9 + 15 = ____	7 • 9 - 7 = ____
9 • 6 = ____	7 • 6 + 57 = ____
23 + 13 = ____	9 • 10 - 57 = ____
29 + 26 = ____	7 + 34 + 21 = ____
20 + 26 = ____	35 - 25 - 9 = ____
37 - 21 = ____	10 + 34 - 7 = ____
11 + 7 = ____	3 • 9 + 8 = ____
15 + 29 = ____	35 + 47 - 35 = ____
38 - 13 = ____	51 + 6 - 10 = ____
39 - 15 = ____	7 • 9 - 51 = ____
5 • 9 = ____	8 • 6 - 48 = ____
30 - 25 = ____	2 • 5 + 37 = ____
24 - 14 = ____	9 • 8 + 7 = ____
12 + 8 = ____	4 • 3 + 40 = ____
3 • 5 = ____	3 • 9 + 22 = ____
29 - 16 = ____	6 • 4 - 17 = ____
17 + 14 = ____	36 + 25 - 6 = ____
2 • 6 = ____	57 - 16 - 11 = ____
9 • 8 = ____	6 + 45 + 11 = ____

Additional tasks - only for math lovers!

$8 \cdot 9 =$ ____	$28 + 13 - 8 =$ ____
$15 + 7 =$ ____	$11 + 27 + 7 =$ ____
$17 - 12 =$ ____	$26 + 19 - 24 =$ ____
$5 \cdot 4 =$ ____	$24 + 9 - 24 =$ ____
$8 + 14 =$ ____	$9 \cdot 5 + 4 =$ ____
$2 \cdot 2 =$ ____	$4 + 25 + 21 =$ ____
$4 \cdot 4 =$ ____	$3 \cdot 3 + 29 =$ ____
$10 + 18 =$ ____	$5 \cdot 7 + 15 =$ ____
$10 - 10 =$ ____	$21 + 20 - 8 =$ ____
$27 - 23 =$ ____	$19 - 7 - 8 =$ ____
$28 - 14 =$ ____	$10 + 10 + 28 =$ ____
$7 + 18 =$ ____	$23 - 9 - 8 =$ ____
$10 \cdot 4 =$ ____	$18 + 5 - 19 =$ ____
$23 - 22 =$ ____	$26 + 12 - 5 =$ ____
$7 \cdot 10 =$ ____	$9 \cdot 3 - 11 =$ ____
$3 \cdot 3 =$ ____	$16 + 3 - 12 =$ ____
$15 + 12 =$ ____	$28 - 6 - 12 =$ ____
$10 \cdot 7 =$ ____	$29 - 8 - 18 =$ ____
$9 \cdot 5 =$ ____	$6 \cdot 2 - 11 =$ ____
$4 \cdot 3 =$ ____	$26 - 15 - 7 =$ ____

Decrypted original text from the previous page:
GREAT PERSON

FIND THE NUMBERS!

18	26
24	56
54	99
36	33
55	62
46	1
16	37
18	35
44	47
25	47
24	12
45	0
5	47
10	79
20	52
15	49
13	7
31	55
12	30
72	62

Mark and count: 49

344916318998856181944715617052
581672901962868547896551175885
709560153486559149721797401839
322176203886207887671663272868
278749404997354630126894323465
994169494533502050747247484117
803518933118725745462083963570
221096187156808882173717719046
285772448577156843499265319025
825419739269862349466248989535
572344155181661516659149838883
754740373123369555608817854980
437793171427432545646982112117

Mark and count: 457

169923961132359451940322935189
516610339558603479882934824803
731644429245197304601327791123
723861760990307148971457476457
488642912786215180318810940457
124880950979354742623236373456
900556457838173905534457427118
880927842866837338281708648892
765836744237419584036648936 17
553768636358294638609243106115
602540481759256281137475976471
536331115457395161822811582828
160891501623457749237283532762

Are you sure? See page 195!

Now draw the visualized picture again with as many details as possible:

TRY TO REMEMBER!

What should you find?

- River: _____
- Country: _____
- Decrypted text: _____

What words should you memorize?

- Object: _____
- Activity: _____

RESULTS - WORDS AND LETTERS

page	number	page	number
18	17	108	16
19	39	109	45
28	13	118	26
29	42	119	43
38	20	128	21
39	34	129	32
48	18	138	15
49	45	139	42
58	26	148	15
59	30	149	38
68	21	158	21
69	46	159	48
78	22	168	22
79	45	169	40
88	21	178	19
89	45	179	26
98	15	188	25
99	39	189	54

RESULTS - FIND THE NUMBERS

page	number		page	number
22 a)	13		112 a)	16
22 b)	9		112 b)	7
32 a)	8		122 a)	10
32 b)	8		122 b)	11
42 a)	21		132 a)	12
42 b)	8		132 b)	9
52 a)	17		142 a)	19
52 b)	10		142 b)	6
62 a)	10		152 a)	12
62 b)	9		152 b)	11
72 a)	21		162 a)	17
72 b)	10		162 b)	10
82 a)	17		172 a)	21
82 b)	16		172 b)	5
92 a)	8		182 a)	15
92 b)	8		182 b)	10
102 a)	13		192 a)	9
102 b)	5		192 b)	7

DECRYPTED CODE

ARE YOU
CURIOUS ABOUT
WHAT YOU FOUND OUT?

HERE YOU CAN WRITE DOWN
THE DECODED TEXT
FOR EACH UNIT!

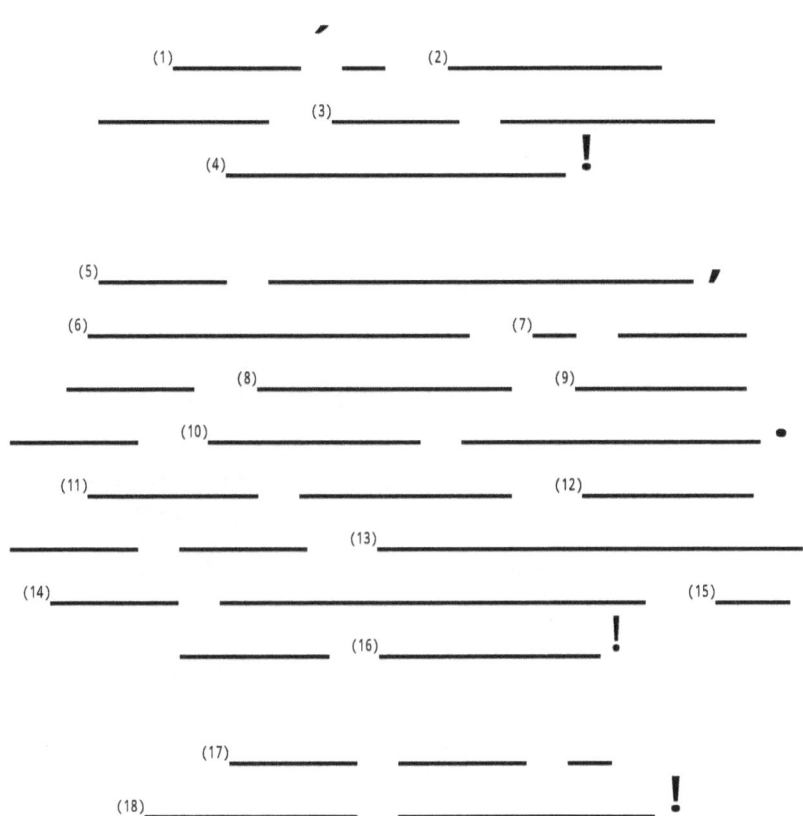

Good luck for your future!

BOOKS OF THE SERIES

www.alexanderhalm.de

SPACE FOR YOUR NOTES